THE BEST JOKES
AND STORIES

THE BEST JOKES AND STORIES

AND
HOW TO TELL THEM

Gene Levin

Writers Club Press
New York Lincoln Shanghai

The Best Jokes and Stories
and
How to Tell Them

Writers Club Press
an imprint of iUniverse, Inc.

For information address:
iUniverse
2021 Pine Lake Road, Suite 100
Lincoln, NE 68512
www.iuniverse.com

ISBN: 0-595-26766-1

Printed in the United States of America

This work is dedicated

to all those who would

share a laugh with others, and

to my wonderful, patient wife, Rose,

who's heard them all a hundred times…

and still laughs.

I am indebted to Gladys, Corinne, Harold, Sy, Frank, Stanley, Bob and everyone else who's enriched my life over the years with jokes and anecdotes. I am grateful for my friendship with the late Joe Gaon, a master raconteur taken from life much too early.

YOU CAN BE A RACONTEUR

You're giving a talk and you want to make the point that it's important to say what you mean and mean what you say; in short, to use the right word. "The Right Word" in the section—America—will make your point unforgettable. Indeed, it's my experience that good speakers lace their messages with humorous anecdotes; the anecdotes—and the points they drive in—will remain in the minds of the audience far longer than the text of one's speech.

But the stories in this collection are not only for speakers—most everyone likes to hear a good joke, well told. Passing along a good story is the time-tested way for a superior salesman to lubricate the interpersonal bond between himself and a potential buyer. Good salesmen—and saleswomen—tell stories well. There is an art to telling a joke; we have all had the experience at one time or another of hearing someone try to tell a joke and fouling it up. For example:

"A circus mouse has fallen in love with the elephant...."

Have you heard this before? No?

"Anyway, the mouse is in love with the elephant...a female elephant...did I mention that? So the circus is in its winter quarters in California...or is it Florida?...Anyway, one night, the mouse climbs up the elephant's leg and just as he thrusts himself into her a coconut...Oh, of course it's Florida!...where was I...Oh! A coconut falls on her head and she grunts, 'Oof!' The mouse disengages and clambers along her back to her ear and says...says....Oh, dammit, I forgot the punch line!"

One turns away, determined at all costs to avoid that would-be jokester for the rest of the evening, because you can bet your pension that sometime later he is going to buttonhole you and gleefully exclaim, "I remembered the punch line. Let me start over."

The purpose of this book is to survey a selection of jokes—the classics as well as those making the rounds today—and to provide suggestions on how to tell them effectively. I have tried to exclude jokes that might offend special groups (except lawyers, who seem to enjoy 'lawyer' jokes more than anyone), nor are there any political jokes; they are mostly self-serving and short-lived. And there are no 'shaggy-dog' stories or one-liners....

Except for the story about the restaurant patron who asks for coffee, but without cream.

The waitress responds, "We're out of cream. Can I bring the coffee without milk?"

The stories I've chosen tend to be midlength or a bit longer. In telling one, you are painting a picture in the listener's mind. As you build your way to the punch line, the listener is building with you. You communicate your enthusiasm, your excitement right up to the punch line which, totally unexpected, shatters that picture. Indeed, the best jokes are those whose punch lines come from a completely unexpected direction. See, for example, Arthritis (America).

As with any endeavor, it is necessary to practice to become a raconteur. It is my experience that one must tell a story at least three times before it is yours. That's what wives and husbands, friends and neighbors are for.

There are several rules in the art of joke-telling.

1. Never start a story unless you are certain of the lines, and especially the punch line.

2. Never, halfway through a story, pause to ask your audience whether they've heard it. Why?

a) If they haven't heard it, you've just broken the spell.

b) If they have heard it and you're telling it well, they'll enjoy your version of the story. Maybe they'll follow up with a story that builds on yours, which you might enjoy hearing.

c) If they have heard it and you're screwing it up, you're pouring salt into the wound you've made in their senses of humor.

3. Don't inhibit yourself. Throw yourself into your presentation. For example, in the story Kibbutz Size, when describing the manager's description of his acreage, point this way and that way excitedly. Act it out!

4. Do not start laughing before you've completed the story.

After having told it a number of times, you should be beyond that.

What about four-letter words? Is it permissible to tell salty jokes in mixed company?

The answer is—maybe. Know your audience. Motion pictures have introduced modern western culture including four letter words, nudity and soft porn to nearly everyone on the planet, save only people—and I do not mean to derogate them—who purposefully restrict their exposure to such. You will be astonished at the likelihood that persons who appear prim laugh quite merrily at a salty joke and indeed, try to top your story with an even saltier one.

But if you're not sure of your audience, start 'tame'. There are some nice, funny, squeaky-clean stories in this collection. They are marked (G) in the Table of Contents. I have loosely followed the motion-picture code, using PG for stories with mild sexual connotation, R for more directly salty jokes and X for the most ribald.

Telling jokes is not the same as giving a lecture, say, in physics. It is an interactive process. As noted before, you are weaving a picture in the minds of your audience; they are taking part in the creative process by helping you construct that picture, right up to the point when you deliver the punch line. You must tailor your content, pace and emphasis to the audience to help them put together the picture that exists clearly in your mind. And speak clearly; your listener should never have to ask you to repeat a smothered punch line.

The story should be amusing, not only to you, but to your audience. If you wish to develop as a raconteur, you should have a good stock of stories of different types, so you can contribute to a social gathering, no matter who is present. Do not relate a joke that may offend someone; have a few standard all-purpose stories at tongue-tip.

By telling your story a number of times, you impress in your memory the exact wording of that joke. This can be important, especially as one approaches the punch line. There should be no extraneous material, no digressions, no need to apologize for having forgotten to inform your audience that the protagonist, in fact, was wearing his trousers backward, or was unusually tall. There's nothing worse than to hear, in the middle of a story, the phrase, "…oh, I forgot to tell you…."

It is frequently a good idea to personalize your story. Instead of opening: "A man who worked in the garment business…." give him a name. "Sammy Feldman had been in the garment business for forty years…." This establishes a picture in the mind of your listener of an elderly, workworn Jewish family man.

I have categorized the following stories, but the selection of groupings is very arbitrary and many of the stories really belong under two or more headings.

How and when should you intrude into a conversation to relate your joke?

Listen for a trigger word. The jokes in this collection are listed in the Contents by words or short phrases that should, if you've prepared yourself, remind you of the entire story. Given the opening, you can recite the classic, "That reminds me of…." Or, just wait for a momentary lull in the conversation. Don't butt in. Have patience. But be alert for the trigger word that will be your key.

What about puns? See The King's Jester.

And what about longer stories? Do you have to memorize them word for word?

Certainly not. With practice, you'll be surprised how the words tumble out in proper order. Lay the foundation, build the house one story at a time, and prepare for the punch line to come.

Note: Suggestions for delivery of many of the jokes are enclosed in brackets, like these []. The underlined material is crucial to the telling. Make sure you get the phrasing straight.

CONTENTS

ADVENTURE

[Reminder: Suggestions are enclosed in brackets, like this one. The underlined material is crucial to the telling.]

1. Shoot the Dog

An American zoo needed three <u>male</u> gorillas but couldn't afford the hundred-thousand dollars to mount a full safari. After much searching, they found a <u>whiskey-drenched hunter</u> who offered to bring in gorillas at only two thousand dollars apiece. A contract was signed, but to make sure this wasn't a hoax, the zoo sent a representative to join the hunter. On the morning of the hunt, the representative was astonished to find the hunter accompanied only by a native bearer pulling an iron-barred wagon and a <u>pit-bull</u>. The hunter was carrying a <u>double-barrelled shotgun</u>.

"<u>I don't understand," the representative said. "What's the dog for?</u>"

"Just follow me and stay out of the way," the hunter grunted, and they ventured into the jungle. Soon enough, the hunter signalled a halt—there, in a high tree, was a male gorilla. The hunter gave the native bearer the shotgun, quietly climbed the tree until he was just behind the gorilla, which had been watching his ascent. The native bearer put a reed to his lips and blowing, imitated the call of the <u>female gorilla in heat</u>. The male, startled, looked around; the hunter pushed him off the branch and the animal landed on the ground on his rump. The dog darted forward, clamped his jaws on the <u>gorilla's genitals</u>, and held tight as the hunter made his way to the ground. The gorilla, unable to move without extreme pain, was soon tied up and bundled into the portable cage.

Off they went in search of more gorillas. Sure enough, they came to a place where there was a gorilla in another tree and the same procedure was carried out. The hunter climbed, the native bearer imitated the mating call of the female and no sooner had the animal been shoved from his perch than the dog swooped in and immobilized it.

As they headed deeper into the jungle to find their third gorilla, the representative asked, "<u>Frankly, I'm astounded. But why do you bother with the shotgun?</u>"

"Maybe you'll see. Just keep out of the way."

After two hours of searching, the hunter again signalled a halt. There, in a treetop, was King Kong, eating a fruit. Again the hunter climbed, again the native bearer blew on his reed and again the hunter gave the gorilla a mighty shove. But the huge gorilla shoved him right back, and as the hunter went tumbling to the ground, he cried out, "<u>Shoot the dog!</u>" [Punch line half-shouted.]

2. Vegas Story

A New Yorker, fed up with the rat race, the tension and pressure, sold everything, jumped into his car and headed west with a huge wad of cash in his pocket. For the first time in years, he felt free! On the fifth day, as he was driving on a highway near Las Vegas, he felt a tug on his right elbow, though he was alone in the car. Then a soft voice called, "Go to Vegas."

<u>This is a miracle! Once in a thousand years, maybe!</u> As he neared the next highway exit, the tug increased and the voice was more urgent, "Get off here. Go to Las Vegas!" [This is whispered loudly.]

Bursting with excitement, he raced off the highway and barrelled along until he saw the first casino. He was about to pull into its parking lot when the voice says, [Again, whisper loudly.] "Not here. Not yet!"

He slowed down for casino after casino, but each time the voice insisted, "Not yet!" As they approached the grandest casino on the strip, the voice said, "This one!" and he screeched to a halt in the parking lot, leaped out of his car and ran headlong into the building. There was a poker table to his left, but the voice said, "No." A Blackjack game on his right, but the voice said, [Whisper excitedly] "No. The dice…the dice!"

He ran up to the dice game, took his bankroll out of his pocket and was about to bet when the voice said, [Excitedly] "Wait! Not yet!" With his heart racing and blood pressure causing his ears to pound, he waited until the dice were passed to him.

"NOW!" the voice bellowed. Dropping his entire savings on the table, he rolled the dice…three and one. Four. He had to roll another four before rolling seven. He closed his eyes, bit his lip and rolled. Four…and three. Seven. He'd crapped out. The voice said, [Softly, with disappointment] "Oh, shit."

3. Lufthansa

The Lufthansa stratoliner's engines fail, one by one, and the pilot skillfully glides down to a smooth landing on the ocean. The pilot stands at the head of the passenger compartment and announces, [A hint of a German accent if you can do it. Note the word order. Practice.] "You see that vee are down on the ocean. It is not to worry so much. Those of you who can shwim, please come forward and leave by the emergency exit onto the right wing; it vill float for a short time."

Half the passengers emerge onto the right wing.

"So," the pilot continues, smiling ruefully. "Those of you who cannot shwim, come forward and step out onto the left wing. It, too, vill float for a short time."

Then, to the passengers on the right wing, he barks out: "Those who can shwim…SHWIM!"

Then, to the passengers on the left wing, he announces, "Those who cannot shwim…thank you for flying Lufthansa."

4. Tip the Whipper

[This is an ethnic joke and should be told with a slight accent.]

Goldfarb, a retired Jew from the Bronx has always wanted to visit Israel, but never had the money. One day he reads in the paper: Cruise to Israel—Fifty dollars!

This he has. He calls the phone number and is told to show up that evening at eleven o'clock, pier 31 in Manhattan, with one valise. He takes a taxi that night to pier 31, which is very dark and totally deserted. Cautiously he walks out onto the pier, further...further...sees no one...then <u>CLOP</u> he's whacked on the back of the head and the next thing he knows he's on a bench inside a ship, chained to an oar with three other men, all rowing for their lives! There are fifty benches, twenty-five on each side of the dark, damp vessel and a catwalk down the middle patrolled by a huge fellow with a twelve-foot bullwhip, which he cracks and snaps.

Goldfarb learns to pull with his oarmates...and the days and nights pass. Goldfarb, despairing of his life, resigns himself to dying in that place when one day he hears a new sound and the men are told to stop rowing. The hatch is opened; daylight pours in and the captain comes down with a large ring of keys.

They've reached Haifa! And after they're all unlocked, the men are escorted up to the deck—the suitcases are all lined up, the gangplank is down and they're free to visit Israel!

Goldfarb goes up to the captain and says, [Bewildered, uncertain tone of voice] "You know, I've never travelled like this before. How much do you tip the whipper?"

5. The Bull's Balls

A traveler to Madrid, about to order dinner in an elegant restaurant, sees that a person dining nearby is enjoying his meal immensely. He asks his waiter, "What is that fellow eating?"

The waiter smiles. "Ah, senor, that is the specialty of the house. Every afternoon there is what you call…the bullfight. And those are the testicles of the bull, garnished and broiled to perfection and served with poached eggs!"

"Well, I'd like to try that also," the traveler says, closing his menu.

"Ah," the waiter sighs. "There is but one bullfight today. I am so sorry. Return tomorrow. I will take your name and the dinner will be prepared."

So the next evening the traveler returns, seats himself and snaps his finger at the waiter, who vanishes into the kitchen and returns with a silver chafing dish. Removing the cover, he spoons the dinner onto the diner's plate.

"But these are very small!" the traveler complains. "The ones I saw yesterday were much larger!"

The waiter nods and replies, apologetically, "I am muy sorry, senor, but sometimes…the bull wins."

AMERICA

6. C.E. Delancey

[This is a double-header…two stories from the lower east side a hundred years ago….]

Isaac and Shmuel put Poland behind them and come to America. They work hard at whatever jobs they can find, but gradually lose touch with each other. Isaac works in a dry-goods store, eventually becomes its manager. Thirty-five years go by like lightning and we find him selling men's clothing for the biggest manufacturer in New York. He's close to retirement, but would like to cap his career by selling to Aberdeen & Bellamy, the fanciest department store in the city. But the Chief Buyer for Aberdeen is <u>C.E.</u>

<u>Delancey</u>, who's harder to get an appointment with than the mayor. But Isaac persists and one fine spring day finds him leaving the elevator with a brand-new briefcase loaded with photographs of the winter line and making his way across plush carpet, past two formidable secretaries and into Delancey's spacious office.

And he is astonished to find that C.E. Delancey is none other than his old friend, Shmuel, from Poland! After much embracing and backslapping and catching up, Isaac asks, "So what's with this C.E. Delancey business?"

His friend responds, "I'm one week in this country and I decide that with a name like Shmuel Mumzberger I'm going nowhere. I look up and I see a sign—Delancey Street. I figure if they name a street after a

Delancey, it must be a good name to have in America. So I change my name to Delancey."

"And the C.E.?"

"Corner Essex."

7. Chicken Soup

[This is a natural follower to #1. Tomashevsky was a real person so you must get his name right.]

Many years ago the Yiddish theaters on the Lower East Side were very popular and one of the great actors was Boris Tomashevsky. It is said that Tomashevsky died suddenly during a performance. The curtain was immediately closed and soon the manager appeared and said, with great sorrow, "It is my sad duty to inform you that the great actor, Boris Tomashevsky is dead!"

An older woman in the balcony yelled down, "Give him chicken soup!"

The manager, startled, stared, then called up, "You don't understand, ma'am; Tomashevsky is dead!"

"Give him chicken soup!" the woman repeated.

"He is dead!" the manager cried. "Chicken soup can't help!"

"It can't hurt!" the woman responded.

8. Skinner

[This requires much practice; the names aren't too important but the rhymes are crucial. You must really throw yourself into the telling. The punch line, 'It was some chap named Skinner!'must be related with delight, just as though you were an English toff at his club.]

Charlie Simmons works for a large British company and travels to America from time to time on business, but hates it and always gets his business done as quickly as possible. "The Yanks are so bloody boring; they have no sense of humor!" he insists at his club.

On his latest trip, however, he meets a salesman who takes him out to dinner. After he's begun to complain about the lack of humor in Yankeeland, the salesman interrupts and tells him the following:

There once was a fellow named Skinner,
who took a young lady to dinner.
By half-past eight they were still at the plate;
by a quarter to ten it was in her.
Not Skinner, the dinner!
Skinner was in 'er before dinner;
he was no beginner!

The Englishman roars with laughter and now he can't wait to get back home to tell this clever joke to the fellows at his club. No sooner has his plane landed at Heathrow than he takes a taxi to his club and finds his buddy Chumly.

"Chumly, old sock, I was completely wrong about the Yanks!" he says, and proceeds to recite:

There once was a fellow named…er Tupper,
who took a young lady to supper.
By half-after eight they were still at the plate;
by a quarter to ten it was up her!
Not the supper! And not Tupper!
It was some chap named Skinner!

9. Not So Fast

On board the huge aircraft carrier Enterprise, a message is received on the bridge. MOTHER OF ENSIGN BROWN DEAD. PLEASE INFORM AND ARRANGE FOR LEAVE.

The captain hands the message to his first mate, Spencer, and tells him to take care of this. Spencer has Brown summoned to the bridge and tells him, "Ensign Brown, <u>we've just learned that your mother is dead</u>. We'll arrange for...."

But Brown is on the deck, fainted away. After Brown is revived and sent down to sick bay to recover from the shock, the captain pulls Spencer into a corner of the bridge and gives him a tongue-lashing. "That was the least sensitive, rottenest way to break the news to that poor sailor! Your mother's dead! If you ever again have occasion to handle that job, be gentle! Break it to him slowly; give him a chance to prepare himself! Now I want you to think over what I just told you!"

Mortified, Spencer nods.

A week later, another message is received from stateside. MOTHER OF ENSIGN JONES DEAD. PLEASE INFORM AND ARRANGE FOR LEAVE.

The captain hands this to Spencer and demands, "Well? Do you know how you're going to handle it this time?"

Spencer, smiling broadly, salutes. "Ay, ay, sir." Taking the microphone in hand, Spencer broadcasts to the entire ship, "All hands on deck! All hands on deck!"

In orderly fashion, the entire crew not engaged in the running of the vessel assemble on the flight deck. Spencer, regarding the neat rows and columns of personnel, calls out over the speaker system: "Those of you whose mothers are living, take one step forward!" As the men comply, Spencer adds, "<u>Not so fast, Jones</u>."

[Again, act out the punch line. Hold up your hand as though you were First Mate Spencer. There's another version of this joke which is the same up to the bawling-out of Spencer by the captain:]

"You don't break hard news like that! Suppose it were the ensign's cat that had died! Suppose the ensign were very attached to the cat. You might call him in and tell him...say, his cat's been on the roof three days and won't come down. Then wait a few hours and inform him that the cat's fallen off the roof and is in the vet's but he's very dehydrated. Then, the next day, you can tell him that the cat died."

When the message comes in regarding Ensign Jones's mother, Spencer has Jones brought up to the bridge, where he informs him: "I'm sorry, Ensign Jones, but your mother's been on the roof for three days…."

10. Marcus Lapidus

[This is an ethnic (Jewish) joke but doesn't require an accent. The name Lapidus must be pronounced 'lap i duss', not Lapeedus!]

Sol and Murray, partners in the very competitive toy business, are concerned about falling sales. One day, Sol picks up a copy of a fashion magazine and reads that this season, only the blackest of suits are in for executives. He tells Murray they have to get themselves black suits if they expect to impress buyers. So off they go on a bright spring day to Marcus Lapidus, the Fashion King of Third Avenue.

Marcus himself waits upon them, takes their measurements, and tells them their suits will be ready the following Tuesday. And they are. Sol and Murray try the suits on…but under the fluorescent lights, it's hard to tell whether these are really black-black, or just light black.

"OK if we step outside in the sunlight?" Marcus, they ask.

"Of course. Suit yourselves! Hah, hah."

Outside, they hold up their arms and turn this way and that, but can't decide whether Marcus's material is really black. Suddenly Sol spots a nun walking toward them. As everyone knows, a nun's habit is absolutely black. As she reaches them, they fall in step, Sol on the left holding his right arm against her habit, Murray on the right, holding his left arm against her habit. Murray says something; the men fall back and the nun continues directly to her nunnery and doesn't stop until she's in the office of the Mother Superior.

"The strangest thing just happened," she says. "I was walking along Third Avenue when two Jewish men wearing dark suits fell in step with me, held up their arms against my sleeves, muttered something in Latin and went into a clothing store."

"But what did they say in Latin?" the Mother Superior asked.

"Marcus Lapidus Fuktus!"

11. By The Numbers

[Straight joke, but requires practice. Tell it at a good clip.]

Introduction: Sometime in the late forties, in an effort to keep the noise level down, inmates in the dining-room of an American prison were forbidden to tell jokes. Since there were a limited number of jokes in circulation and they all knew those stories, they decided to give each joke a number. During the meal, if someone wanted to tell a joke, all he had to do was recite that number and he'd get his response from his fellow-inmates.

Sometimes the response was meager.

"What happened?" a new inmate asked. "I call out forty-two and no one laughed."

"You didn't tell it right."

12. Crazy Professor

[The three 'facts' don't matter; use any three you like. This is a good, clean joke for an audience including teachers.]

Checking out the intelligence of his new class, a professor says: "If the diameter of the Earth is about eight thousand miles, and the highest mountain is Mt. Everest, and the cost of an ice-cream soda is $2.50, how old am I?"

One student in the rear calls out, "Forty-eight."

The professor, astonished, says, "You're right. How'd you figure it out?"

"Oh, I got a brother home, he's twenty-four and he's only half-crazy."

13. Drink First

On a transcontinental flight, the passengers have endured unusual turbulence and as the plane approaches Kennedy airport in New York, the pilot gets on the public address system. "Please fasten your seat belts now. We'll be landing in about twenty minutes. Thanks for flying with us and enjoy your stay."

Forgetting to turn off the P.A. system, the pilot says to the co-pilot, "That was the roughest trip I've ever experienced. When I get down, all I want is a double scotch and the best woman in town."

A stewardess in the rear of the plane, hearing this and realizing he forgot to turn off the P.A. system, starts rushing up toward the cockpit. Halfway up the aisle, a little old lady sticks her cane out and says, "No hurry, darlin'; he wants a drink first!"

14. True Story

This is a true story—no joke!

There's a TV station in Michigan where the anchorperson is a woman and the weather forecaster is a man. One evening he predicted substantial snow for the next day; it never happened. That night, the anchorwoman, after finishing her portion, turned to the forecaster and asked, "So, Bob, where's the eight inches you promised me last night?"

Not only did HE have to leave the set; half the camera crew did too; they were laughing so hard!

15. Second Language

[An excellent joke for an audience of teachers.]

A mother cat was walking down the sidewalk with her kittens trailing behind, when suddenly a large dog jumped out from behind a fence.

"Woof!" said the cat, and the dog scampered away.

She turned to her kittens and said, "You see, it pays to know a second language."

16. Farmer

[Make sure of your audience before telling this one.]

A New England farmer hired a high school senior from New York to do chores for the summer. As the time approached when the boy would be returning to the city, the farmer said, "Well, I was mighty satisfied with what you done here this summer, and we're goin' to celebrate with a party!"

"Great!" the boy replies.

"I wanna warn you," the farmer continues, "there's gonna be drinkin'!"

"Oh, I can hold a few beers down," the boy says.

"And there's gonna be cussin'!"

"I can handle that," the boy replies.

"But there's gonna be fightin'!" the farmer warns.

"I can take care of myself," the boy replies, flexing his biceps.

"An' there's gonna be sex!"

"Wow! I'm sure ready for that!" the boy says eagerly. "What should I wear?"

"No matter," the farmer says. "Just gonna be you and me there."

17. Mayhem

[Great story for housewives.]

One afternoon a man came home from work to find total mayhem in his house. His three children were outside, still in their pajamas, playing in the mud, with empty food boxes and wrappers strewn all around the front yard. The door of his wife's car was open, as was the front door to the house.

Proceeding inside, he found an even bigger mess. A lamp had been knocked over and the throw rug was wadded against one wall. In the front room the TV was loudly blaring a cartoon channel, and the family room was strewn with toys and various items of clothing. In the kitchen, dishes filled the sink, breakfast food was spilled on the counter, dog food was spilled on the floor, a broken glass lay under the table and a small pile of sand was spread by the back door. He quickly headed up the stairs, stepping over toys and more piles of clothes, looking for his wife. Surely something serious had happened. He found her lounging in the bedroom, still curled in the bed in her pajamas, reading a novel.

She looked at him, smiled, and asked how his day had gone. He looked at her bewildered and asked, "What happened here today?"

She again smiled and answered, "You know every day when you come home and ask me what in the world did I do today?"

"Yes," was his incredulous reply.

She answered, "Well, today I didn't do it."

18. The Right Word

[This story has a moral—Use the Right Word!]

An executive walks into a doctor's office early in the morning and asks to be castrated. The doctor, surprised, sits him down and starts to try to talk him out of it, but the man, in a hurry, says, "Listen, this is a simple procedure; let's not make it into a big, expensive deal. Just do it."

So the doctor performs the procedure and the man is sitting in the waiting room, recuperating, when another man walks in and asks to be circumcised.

"That's the word!" the first one exclaims.

19. All the Feed on the Wagon

[Great story for ministers, rabbis, chronic speechmakers. Make sure you have the punch line down.]

In Minnesota the winters can get rough, with huge accumulations of snow. One Sunday morning, with snow accumulations of three and four feet, only one man showed up at a rural church. After finishing the prayer portion of the service, the minister announced that, "Since only one person has shown up, I won't bother delivering my sermon."

The parishioner held up his hand and said, "Well, now, that don't seem right. I'm a farmer, and sometimes a big snow comes up and catches my herd out in the field. I load up a wagon with feed and bring it out to them, so they don't starve. Sometimes only one cow shows up for the feed; just because it's one cow, shouldn't I see that she gets what she needs?"

The minister nods, steps up to the podium and delivers a sermon that runs well over an hour. Then, stepping down, he asks, "Well, how was that?"

The farmer says, "Well, just because only one cow shows up, I don't make her eat all the feed on the wagon!"

[You can follow that up with…"And speaking of hunger…."]

A New Yorker is visiting his Vermont cousin, a farmer. They're standing out by the chicken coops when a rooster starts chasing one of the hens. The farmer chuckles and says, "Watch this."

Reaching into his pocket, he pulls out a handful of feed and tosses it toward the rooster, which brakes sharply and starts pecking. The New Yorker shakes his head and says, "I just hope I never get that hungry."

20. Parrot

An older gentleman is sitting on a park bench and a hippie comes along and drops himself onto the other end of the bench. The kid has rings and jeweled pins in his nose, eyebrows, cheek, earlobes, spiked, multicolored hair and is dressed accordingly. The gentleman stares long enough so that the kid snaps, "What's the matter, old man? You stuck in the middle ages? Get a life!"

The gentleman says, "I confess…I was staring because…in my youth, I once had sex with a parrot and I was wondering whether you might be my son."

21. Wife Away from Home

[Must be told with enthusiasm. Pronounce the punch line very clearly and exactly; the word button must be the last word spoken.]

A traveller finds himself in a Greyhound bus station at a very late hour; the station is completely deserted, there's no newsstand and he has nothing to read. He sees, along one wall, a rack of modern-looking vending machines and walks over. The first machine advertises:

Shoe-shine, 25 cents.

Pretty cheap. He steps into the designated holes, drops in a quarter and pushes the button. Whirr, brush, shirr, snap…when the machine stops, he takes out his feet and his shoes shine like new! The next machine advertises:

Haircut, one dollar.

How can a machine give a haircut? But he needs one, and has nothing better to do, so he slips in a dollar, puts his head in the aperture in the machine, presses the button and is treated to a series of whirrs, clicks and clacks, rubbings, sprayings, shavings and brushings and when the machine stops, looks at himself in the mirror. He is astonished! This machine has given him a forty-dollar styling! He tries every machine, and is delighted at the results. The final machine in the row advertises:

Your Wife Away From Home—One dollar.

Well, he's alone in the station. He puts in a dollar bill, opens his fly, inserts himself into the aperture and presses the button…and gives out a scream!

Withdrawing his pecker, he sees, neatly sewn on the end, a button.

22. Denise, DeNephew

[A good, classic all-purpose joke.]

A businessman whose wife is expecting to give birth any day is called away on business to Africa. Unfortunately, communications are very poor and when he finally flies home he telephones from the airport to see how she's doing. A message informs him that she's in the hospital, and that's where the businessman goes by taxi. The doctor meets him in the waiting room, all smiles.

"Your wife had twins, a boy and a girl! Congratulations!"

"Wonderful!" he exclaims. "What are their names?"

"Well, your wife was under deep anesthesia, but her brother provided the names."

"You let my brother-in-law, who hardly knows his own middle name, name my children!" the businessman snaps. "Well?"

"The girl he named Denise...."
Relieved, the businessman nods. "Denise...that's a nice name."
The doctor continues, "And the boy...Denephew."

23. Second Grade Essay

[Every region has an exclusive, wealthy enclave. New York has several; I use King's Point. This is a straight, clean story—very effective if the current topic happens to be wealth.]

Tiffany Gotrocks, a second grader who lived in Kings Point, had to write an essay about a poor family. This is the essay she wrote:

Once upon a time, there was a poor family. The father was poor, the mother was poor and all the children were poor. The cook was poor, the maid was poor, the chauffeur was poor, the gardener was poor....

24. To My First Grandchild

[This follows the preceding story very naturally. Slip it in quickly....]

A wealthy man had three married sons, but no grandchildren. He was getting impatient, so he invited the boys and their wives to dinner. He bowed his head to say grace, then continued, "I want it to be known that, to my first grandchild, I intend to give a hundred thousand dollars and to his parents, to defray the cost of raising him or her, an additional hundred thousand."
He raised his head to find himself alone at the table.

25. Logging Camp

[Clean story—Moral: Don't judge a book by its cover.]

The manager of a logging camp out west is in his office wading through paperwork when the door opens and a small, stringy fellow walks in carrying a big, double-bladed ax and asks for a job.

The manager smiles, and says, "I'd like to help you out, but…well, you're not built for the kind of work we do here."

"Try me," the man insists. "Show me a tree you want cut down."

To get the fellow off his back, the manager takes him outside and points to a pine tree. "Try that one," he says, and returns to his office. Ten minutes later, he hears a crash, some furious chopping, then silence. The door opens and there's the stringy fellow.

"Done," he says. "And I took off the branches."

The manager looks outside and is impressed. "Good job," he admits. "But in this camp, we don't really cut pine. We cut bigger trees. Why don't you…."

"Show me one," the woodsman insists.

"Okay," shrugs the manager. "See that oak over there? About three feet across…."

Without a word, the woodsman scurries off in that direction and the manager retreats to his office to continue his paperwork. Twenty minutes later there's a huge crash and furious chopping and the door opens and there's the woodsman again!

"Down and the branches off."

The manager goes outside and sure enough, the oak is down and its branches lopped off perfectly.

"Well, you did that nice and neat," he says, "but I'll tell you the truth…in this camp, we only cut <u>sequoia</u>, the giant redwood! We work in crews of three and it's a full day job just to strip the branches, let alone bringing the trunk down. Why don't you…."

"Show me one," the woodsman demands.

The manager, shaking his head, points to a tree marked for cutting and returns to his office, certain that the woodsman will quietly vanish.

An hour and a half later, there's a tremendous crash and the earth shakes. The manager dashes outside and is astounded to see the huge tree on its side with its many branches removed and lying neatly nearby. The woodsman is there, leaning on his ax.

The manager says, "I don't believe it! Where did you learn to cut like that?"

"In the Sahara Forest."

"Huh? You mean the Sahara Desert?"

The woodsman smiles and replies, "That's what they call it now."

[Emphasize now!]

26. Almost Got Caught

[This is one of a category of what are called in academia 'Dean Jokes'.]

A dean was on a committee to prepare a long report the college needed for re-accreditation. One day, after meeting for several hours, the dean, fatigued, saw that it was four o'clock and suggested that they break for the day. Just then the president entered, saw that the committee was about to disband and announced, "I put in a full nine-to-five day as president, and I expect no less of all of you."

The members of the committee sat down and continued working. The next afternoon at four o'clock, as they continued their work, the dean looked out the window and saw the president leaving. "He's gone. Let's split," he suggested, and soon he was in his car driving home. Entering his house, he didn't see his wife in the kitchen, but when he went upstairs and opened the door to the bedroom, there's his wife in bed with the president! Trembling, he silently closed the door, tiptoed downstairs, returned to his car and left to spend the next hour in the library.

The next afternoon the committee again was meeting and again the president was seen leaving at four o'clock. "He's gone," said another committee member. "Let's go."

"Not me," said the dean. "Yesterday I almost got caught."

27. Half a Grapefruit

[Good story. Pronounce the word whores as <u>hooers</u> for an authentic sound. For effect, the punch line is condensed to an absolute minimum of words. Therefore, don't bother with '<u>did</u> she play for'.]

A fellow goes to the produce counter in a supermarket and asks the young man who's working there for a half grapefruit.

"You don't buy a half grapefruit," snaps the young man. "You buy a whole grapefruit, take it home and cut it in half."

But the man insists on buying a half grapefruit and the produce man, grudgingly, walks over to the manager's office to pass the problem to him, <u>not realizing that the man is following him</u>. Poking his head inside the door, he says, "There's some jerk out there wants to buy a half grapefruit." Then, from the corner of his eye, he sees the customer right behind him and says, "And <u>this gentleman</u> would like to buy the other half."

The manager okays the purchase, then calls the produce man back. "You know, I heard the entire exchange out there. You thought very quickly. I'm opening a branch store in Canada; how'd you like to manage it?"

"Canada?" the produce man laughs. "All they have up in Canada is hooers and hockey players."

Bristling, the manager says, "<u>I'll have you know my wife comes from Canada</u>."

"Really?" the produce man replies with raised eyebrows. "What team she play for?"

28. Fried Eggs

[You must act this out, illustrating with your hands. Tell it at a good pace; don't drag it out.]

Fellow walks into a lingerie store to buy a sexy nightie set for his wife.
"What size bra?" the female clerk asks.
Puzzled, the fellow grunts, "No idea."
"Well, are we talking…grapefruits?" [Fingers spread wide apart.]
Shakes his head. "Nah."
"Oranges?" [Smaller handspread.]
"Nah."
"Lemons?" she asks hopefully. [With a sorry look, give up on the hand display.]
"Nope."
In a small voice, "Eggs?"
[With a mournful look] "Yeah. Fried!"

29. Pass the Salt

A New York couple, both professionals, have been married for some years and the wife is not getting pregnant. They go to a doctor who examines them separately and finds them healthy. Calling them into his office, he explains:
"The problem seems to be that you're both so busy with your careers you're peaking in sexual desire at different times. There's no…coming together, if you get my drift. The next time you both feel amorous at the same moment, no matter what you're involved in, you must stop and have sex."

Three months later, the couple sees the doctor…she's definitely pregnant—nausea, soreness in her breasts, hot flashes. But she's beaming.

"Well," the doctor says. "I'm glad it worked out. Tell me the circumstances."

The husband volunteers, somewhat red-faced, "Well, it was during dinner. I asked her to pass the salt. She was wearing a push-up bra, very low-cut. She leaned over and smiled. I was overwhelmed and we did it right there. It was very messy."

"Messy?" the doctor asks.

"Well, first I kicked over the centerpiece and spilled a load of flowers into the bride's soup. Then my wife's shoes went flying and hit the drum and the band struck up "Go Man Go" and the bride started to cry and the whole wedding party formed a conga line around our table…."

[The closing paragraph should be told with enthusiasm.]

30. Lion and Lamb

A world-famous political advisor and international negotiator retired and decided to create and operate a zoo. A reporter, hearing of this, visited the zoo and was astounded to see in the same cage, lying side-by-side, a lion and a lamb.

"But this is amazing!" he gasped. "How does it work?"

"Simple," said his host. "Every day a new lamb."

31. Arthritis

A priest is sitting on a park bench reading a newspaper when a raggedly-dressed, unshaven bum with an aura of alcohol drops onto the other end of the bench, groans and adjusts his body to minimize his apparent discomfort. He pulls out a much-folded newspaper, blinks, grimaces and starts to read it. The priest, disgusted by the presence of this whiskey-sotted vagrant ignores him until the bum leans over and asks,

"Excuse me but what causes arthritis?"

The priest cannot hold back. He declares, "It's caused mainly by failing to wash and shave, by drinking to excess and ignoring dental care, by masturbation and sexual indulgence of the most evil kind and by consorting with the vilest of people."

"Ah!" the bum says, nodding. Pointing to his newspaper, he says, "I see here that the pope has it."

32. Tampax

An eight-year-old boy walks into a drugstore with his four-year-old brother in hand. "I want to buy a box of Tampax," he says to the druggist, pulling out a worn dollar bill.

"And what do you want this for?" the druggist asks.

"Oh, it's not for me; it for my brother here," the boy says. "The ad on TV said that with Tampax you can swim and ride a bicycle, and Johnnie can't do either of those things."

33. Kindergarten

[This is a tricky one—you have to remember the sequence of problems in order. Wrong feet—Not my boots—brother's—mittens in boot-toes. Pause before the final punch line, which is delivered blandly.]

A teacher was helping one of her kindergarten students put on his boots. He had asked for help and she could see why. With her pulling and him pushing, the boots still didn't want to go on.

When the second boot was on, she had worked up a sweat. She almost whimpered when the little boy said, 'Teacher, they're on the wrong feet.'

She looked and sure enough, they were.

It wasn't any easier pulling the boots off than it was putting them on but she managed to keep her cool as together they worked to get the boots back on—this time on the right feet.

He then announced, 'These aren't my boots.'

She bit her tongue rather than get right in his face and scream, 'Why didn't you say so?' like she wanted to. Once again she struggled to help him pull the ill-fitting boots off.

He then said, 'They're my brother's boots. My Mom made me wear them.'

She didn't know if she should laugh or cry. She mustered up the grace and courage she had left to wrestle the boots on his feet again. Then she said, 'Now, where are your mittens?'

He said, 'I stuffed them in the toes of my boots....'

Her insurance doesn't cover therapy.

34. Fire at Nuclear Plant

A fire had erupted at a nuclear power plant and quickly all the firemen and apparatus in the area converged to put it out. But despite their best efforts, the fire raged and the firemen couldn't get their streams of water and chemicals to its heart, deep within the plant. The chief was frightened that the core would melt down and ordered his men to try harder...to get closer...to risk anything to get cooling water to the heart of the fire. But they couldn't! The heat was so intense their hoses disintegrated before they could get water near the core. Phone calls went out to all cities in the area to send men and equipment and they came but were still unable to attack the fire at its heart.

Suddenly, from a small village some twenty miles away, a lone pumper came tearing along the road at eighty miles per hour, heading directly toward the flaming power plant. Men scattered as the vehicle tore directly into the ring of fire at top speed with its pumps going full-blast…and within minutes, the fire began to subside and soon it was out completely.

The fire crew, faces and hands black from smoke and soot, emerged from their pumper and were greeted with cries of relief and prayers and promises that their heroism would be recognized…and it was. Within a week, the governor had them all to the capitol where they were given the highest honors, medals and a check for fifty thousand dollars.

"What are you heroes going to do with that fifty thousand dollars?" a reporter asked.

The chief replied, "Well, first thing I'm gonna do is get new brakes for the pumper!"

35. No Time for Herself

[Make sure you have all the 'indulgences' before you start this one.]

The phone rings in Tiffany's California Ranch house at nine-thirty in the morning. She picks it up and as she sips her second coffee, says,

"Elizabeth? Golf? Today? Oh, I can't; I just can't. I have a beauty parlor at ten-thirty, then I'm having my legs waxed at eleven-forty-five, then Ambrose is doing my nails at one o'clock and I have a tanning session scheduled for two and a private tennis lesson with Raoul at three-thirty and I'm having my gown fitted at five. I'm telling you, Lizzie, I'm so busy I just have no time for myself!"

36. Speeding

A police officer pulls a guy in a sports car over for speeding and has the following exchange:

Officer: May I see your driver's license?

Driver [sullenly]: I don't have one. It was suspended when I got my 5th DWI.

Officer: [Eyes narrowing suspiciously] May I see the owner's card for this vehicle?

Driver: It's not my car. I stole it.

Officer: The car is stolen?

Driver: That's right. But come to think of it, I think I saw the owner's card in the glove box when I was putting my gun in there.

Officer: There's a gun in the glove box?

Driver: Yes sir. That's where I put it after I shot and killed the woman who owns this car and stuffed her in the trunk.

Officer: [alarmed] There's a BODY in the TRUNK?!?!?

Driver: Yes, sir.

Hearing this, the officer immediately called his captain. The car was quickly surrounded by police, and the captain approached the driver to handle the tense situation:

Captain: Sir, can I see your license?

Driver: [calmly] Sure. Here it is.

It was valid.

Captain: Whose car is this?

Driver: It's mine, officer. Here's the owner's card.

The driver owned the car.

Captain: Could you slowly open your glove box so I can see if there's a gun in it?

Driver: Yes, sir, but there's no gun in it.

Sure enough, there was nothing in the glove box.

Captain: Would you mind opening your trunk? I was told you said there's a body in it.

Driver: No problem.

Trunk is opened; no body.

Captain: I don't understand it. The officer who stopped you said you told him you didn't have a license, stole the car, had a gun in the glove box, and that there was a dead body in the trunk.

Driver: Yeah, I'll bet the lying s.o.b. told you I was speeding, too!

37. Halloween

A couple was invited to a swanky <u>masked</u> Halloween Party. The wife got a terrible headache and told her husband to go to the party alone. He, being a devoted husband, protested, but she argued and said she was going to take some aspirin and go to bed, and there was no need of his good time being spoiled by not going. So he <u>took his costume</u> and away he went.

The wife, after sleeping soundly for one hour, awakened without pain. As it was still early, she decided to go to the party. Since her husband did not know what her costume was, she thought she would have some fun watching him to see how he acted when she was not with him. She joined the party and soon spotted her husband cavorting around on the dance floor, dancing with every nice woman he could, copping a little feel here and a little kiss there. His wife sidled up to him. As she was a rather seductive babe herself, he left his partner high and dry and devoted his time to the new stuff that had just arrived.

She let him go as far as he wished; naturally, since he was her husband. Finally he whispered a little proposition in her ear and she agreed, so off they went to one of the cars and had sex. Just before unmasking at midnight, she slipped away, went home, put the costume away and got into bed, wondering what kind of explanation he would make for his behavior.

She was sitting up reading when he came in and she asked how the party was. He said, "Oh, the same old thing. You know I never have a good time when you're not there."

Then she asked, "Did you dance much?"

He replied, "I'll tell you, I never even danced one dance. When I got there, I met Pete, Bill Brown and some other guys, so we went into the den and played poker all evening. But you won't believe what happened to the guy I lent my costume to!"

38. Smart Machine

A nun was going to Chicago. She went to the airport and sat down waiting for her flight. She looked over in the corner and saw one of those weight machines that tells your weight and fortune. So, she thought to herself, "I'll give it a try just to see what it tells me."

She went over to the machine and put her nickel in and out came a card that said, "You're a nun and weigh 128 lb., and you are going to Chicago, Illinois."

She sat back down and thought about it. She told herself it probably tells everyone the same thing, but decided to try it again. She went back to the machine and put her nickel in. Out came a card that read, "You're a nun, weigh 128 lb., you're going to Chicago, Illinois and you are going to play a fiddle."

The nun said to herself, "I know that's wrong, I have never played a musical instrument in my life."

She sat back down. From nowhere a cowboy came over and set his fiddle case down next to her. Taking out the instrument, he played a few tunes, then, with a smile, handed it to her and showed her how to play some scales and in short order had her playing a tune.

Startled, she looked back at the machine and said, "This is incredible. I've got to try it again."

Back to the machine, she put her nickel in and another card came out. It said, "You're a nun, you weigh 128 lb., you're going to Chicago, Illinois and you're going to break wind."

Now the nun knows the machine is wrong. "I've never broke wind in public a day in my life."

She tripped getting off the scale and broke wind.

Stunned, she sat back down and looked at the machine. She said to herself, "This is truly unbelievable! I've got to try it again." She went back to the machine, put her nickel in and collected the card.

It read, "You're a nun, you weigh 128 lb., you have fiddled and farted around and missed your plane to Chicago."

39. Rolls-Royce

This man in a Volkswagen Beetle pulls up next to a guy in a Rolls Royce at a stop sign. Their windows are open and he yells at the guy in the Rolls:

"Hey, you got a telephone in that Rolls?"

The guy in the Rolls says, "Yes, of course I do."

"I got one too…see?"

"Uh, huh, yes, that's very nice."

"You got a fax machine?"

"Why, actually, yes, I do."

"I do too! See? It's right here!"

"Uh-huh."

The light is just about to turn green and the guy in the Volkswagen says, "So, do you have a double bed in back there?"

And the guy in the Rolls says, "NO! Do you?"

"Yep, got my double bed right in back here. See?!"

The light turns and the man in the Volkswagen takes off. Well, the guy in the Rolls is not about to be one-upped, so he goes immediately to a customizing shop and orders them to put a double bed in back of his car.

About two weeks later, the job is finally done and he picks up his car and drives all over town looking for the Volkswagen. He finally finds it parked alongside the road so he pulls his Rolls up next to it. The windows on the Volkswagen are all fogged up and he feels a little awkward about it, but he gets out of his newly modified Rolls and taps on the foggy window of the Volkswagen. The man in the Volkswagen finally opens the window a crack and peeks out.

The Rolls-guy says, "Hey. Remember me?"

"Yeah, yeah, I remember you. What's up?"

"Check this out…I got a double bed installed in my Rolls."

And the man in the Volkswagen snaps, "YOU GOT ME OUT OF THE SHOWER TO TELL ME THAT?!"

ANIMALS

40. Football

[Save this one for autumn—football season.]

The animals in the jungle were playing football, with the elephant as referee. At half-time, the score was 42-0; no one could stop the hippopotamus. Every time the hippo's team got the ball, they gave it to him and he scored.

The second half started and once again the lion passed the ball to the hippo, who began his charge downfield. Suddenly the hippo went down with a thundering crash and a cloud of dust. The giraffe raced over to see who'd tackled him; it was the centipede!

"Wow! Where were you in the first half?" the giraffe demanded.

"I was putting on my sneakers."

41. Lion

The lion, sauntering through his domain, encountered the monkey and roared, "Who is the most fearsome king of the jungle?"

"Y…you are," the monkey chattered, shaking with fright.

The lion nodded and continued on his way until he encountered the giraffe. Again he roared, "Who is the most fearsome king of the jungle?"

The giraffe (unable to speak as it has no voice) bent its neck to the ground and pointed toward the lion, who grunted his approval and continued his stroll until he met the elephant. "Who is the most fearsome king of the jungle?" he roared.

The elephant wrapped his thick trunk around the lion's body, picked the beast up in the air and tossed him a dozen feet into a thornbush. Scratched, aching and in pain from the thorns, the lion carefully eased his way out of the bush and whimpered, "Well, just because you don't know the answer you don't have to get mad!"

[The punch line is delivered meekly, with mock pain.]

42. Rabbit's Thesis

[This is an academic joke, most appreciated by graduate students and untenured professors.]

Wilbur Rabbit was sitting in a clearing in front of a huge cave, pecking away on a typewriter. Renard the fox came along, eyed the rabbit, and asked, "What are you doing?"

"Typing my thesis," the rabbit replied, not missing a keystroke.

"Oh? What's it about?"

"It's titled: WHY RABBITS EAT FOXES."

"That's stupid! Rabbits don't eat foxes," Renard said, already salivating. "Foxes eat rabbits."

"Speak to my advisor," Wilbur said, pointing to the cave. The fox entered the cave and moments later, one could hear sounds of altercation, grunting, a yelp, some crunching and then silence. Wilbur Rabbit kept typing.

Presently a wolf came along, eyed the plump rabbit and asked, "What are you doing?" as it dropped to its belly and eased closer.

"Typing my thesis," the rabbit replied.

"Oh? And what's that about?" the wolf asked.

"It's title is: WHY RABBITS EAT WOLVES."

"How dumb! Rabbits don't eat wolves. Wolves eat rabbits," as the wolf moved closer.

"Ask my thesis advisor," the rabbit said, pointing to the cave.

The wolf, perhaps thinking to bring more than just one rabbit back to its den, entered the cave. Promptly there came the unmistakable noise of combat, snarling, a roar and then…silence.

Wilbur Rabbit kept typing and now a huge bear shuffled into the clearing in front of the cave. "What are you doing?" the bear demanded.

"Typing my thesis," Wilbur replied.

"Oh? And what's your thesis?"

"It's titled: WHY RABBITS EAT BEARS," Wilbur said, "and if you don't agree, talk to my advisor." Pointing to the cave's mouth, he continued typing.

The bear, perhaps thinking this would make a fine cave for his upcoming hibernation, swaggered inside and now there came from within the sound of a major war. Bellows of rage, roars, poundings and thumpings and finally the sound of bones being broken. Then silence, except for Wilbur Rabbit's typing.

Toward dusk, a reporter came into the clearing and, spying the rabbit, asked what it was doing.

"Typing my thesis," Wilbur said.

"And what is your thesis?"

"WHY RABBITS EAT FOXES, WOLVES AND BEARS."

"What an interesting title," the reporter said, jotting down some notes. "Could you tell me more?"

"I'll let you speak to my advisor," the rabbit said and, rising, he led the way into the cave. Near the mouth, the reporter noticed a small pile of bones. Further in, there was a larger pile of bones. And near the rear of the cave was a very large pile of bones. And beyond that, on a wide ledge, a great lion lay on its side, snoring. The rabbit whispered, "You see, the important thing isn't the title of the thesis; it's picking the right advisor."

43. Sex with a Sheep

[Basically a lawyer joke.]

There were two Vermont farmers, neighbors, who weren't overly fond of each other. One day in the early spring, before the border of trees separating their farms were in leaf, Jed looks out from the top floor of his house and sees his neighbor Will in his field having sex with a sheep. Not only is he having sex; the animal has twisted herself around and is licking Will's bottom.

That's all Jed needs; in an instant he's on the phone to the sheriff and in no time at all, Will's been arrested and put in jail.

The local lawyer reviews Will's situation, shakes his head and admits this case is beyond his abilities. "You're going to have to get a big-shot lawyer from the city. Now, I know two lawyers who'd take this case, but they don't come cheap. You can only afford one.

"Stu Thompson is the best courtroom lawyer in the state. He can talk the ears off a statue. Mike Skinner is okay on his feet; his specialty is jury-selection. Which one do you want?"

Will thinks a minute, then says, "Get Skinner."

Two weeks later the case comes to trial. The sheriff testifies: "Not only did I see the defendant, William Shortly, having intercourse with a sheep; the sheep was bent around and was licking Will's bare bottom!"

In the jury box, one juror turns to his neighbor and whispers, "Yeah, a good sheep'll do that."

44. Penguins

A motorcycle cop is hidden behind a sign, keeping an eye out for speeders. Along comes a pickup truck and...what's that in back...looks like a bunch of penguins! He roars out, comes alongside the truck and motions for the driver to pull over.

Sure enough, there are a dozen penguins in the rear of the truck. "Where you headin' with those penguins, fellah?" he demands.

"Jus' takin' them for a ride, officer."

"Look, I ain't going to ask how they came to be in your possession, and I ain't going to ask you what you know about taking care of penguins, but I am tellin' you this: take them to the zoo. Today. Now. That's where penguins belong."

"Yes, sir," and the pickup truck left.

The very next day, the motorcycle cop is stationed at the same location, and along comes the same pickup truck…and in the rear, the same load of penguins! He roars out, pulls the driver over and leans into the cab.

"Didn't I tell you to take those penguins to the zoo?"

"I did, officer, and they had a great time. Today we're going to a movie."

45. Cow/horse

[Before starting this one, make sure you have your reasons straight.]

A New Yorker who'd never been out of Manhattan visited his cousin, who owned a farm in Vermont. One day he called his cousin over and, pointing out into a field, asked, "Why doesn't that cow have horns?"

The cousin squinted, pursed his lips, inserted a fresh straw of hay between his teeth and answered reflectively, "Well, some kinds of cows don't have horns. And some, we have to take the horns off because them cows are aggressive. With some cows the horns come in late…but the reason why that cow don't have horns is because that cow is a horse."

46. Dead Donkey

[This naturally follows Cow/horse.]

A city boy moved to the country and bought a donkey from an old farmer for $100.00. The farmer agreed to deliver the donkey the next day, but when he showed up, the farmer said, "Sorry son, but I have some bad news, the donkey died."

The boy replied, "Well then, just give me my money back."

The farmer said, "Can't do that. I went and spent it already."

The boy said, "OK then, just unload the donkey."

The farmer asked, "What ya gonna do with him?"

The boy said, "I'm going to raffle him off."

Farmer: " You can't raffle off a dead donkey!"

The boy: "Sure I can. Watch me. I just won't tell anybody he is dead."

A month later the farmer met up with the boy and asked, "What happened with that dead donkey?"

Smiling, the boy replied, "I raffled him off. I sold 500 tickets at two dollars apiece and made a profit of $898.00."

The farmer asked, "Didn't anyone complain?"

The boy: "Just the guy who won. So I gave him his two dollars back."

The boy grew up and eventually held an executive position at Enron.

47. Sincerely, the Cat

[This is one of the better ones gleaned from a massive sweep of ten thousand jokes from around the world, a project that originated at the University of Herfordshire in Britain in 2001. Some of the entries were reprinted in the New York Times on January 27, 2002. This one requires some practice.]

To tell the weather: Go to your back door and look for the dog. If the dog is at the door and he is wet, it's probably raining. But if the dog is standing there really soaking wet, it is probably raining really hard. If the dog's fur looks like it's been rubbed the wrong way, it's probably windy. If the dog has snow on his back, it's probably snowing. Of course, to be able to tell the weather like this, you have to leave the dog outside all the time, especially if you expect bad weather.

Sincerely, the Cat.

ATHLETICS

48. Partition

[You can introduce the following with: "The best part of golf is the jokes..."]

At a fancy golf club, they're renovating the locker rooms and they've torn down the wall separating the men's and women's locker rooms. Unfortunately they only had enough wallboard to make a partition from the ceiling down to waist-level and that's how they left it for the weekend.

Three women are standing on their side of the wallboard when a nude man strolls by on the other side. All three peer closely. One says, "Well, it's not my husband."

The second nods, "And it's not my husband."

The third woman says, "Why, he doesn't even belong to the club!"

49. Golf Balls in Attic

A man in his seventies decided, on a rainy day, to clean out the attic. Up there, he spotted a chest he'd never noticed. Opening it, to his surprise, he found three golf balls and a thick wad of ten dollar bills.

"Louise!" he called down to his wife. "You'll never guess what I found up here."

She joined him and after some minutes, said, "John...I...I don't know what to say. I guess I'd better confess. I haven't been completely faithful to you. Every time I...strayed, I put a golf ball in this chest."

Taken aback, John refrained from giving her a tongue-lashing. After all, three...accidents...in fifty years of marriage wasn't all that bad. "But...what about the bundle of ten-dollar bills?" he asked.

"Oh. Whenever I got a dozen balls, I sold them for ten dollars."

50. Scot at Yankee Game

[The punch line should be delivered with a distinct Scottish burr. "Walk with prrride, man...."]

McTavish came to America and was taken by his cousin to his first baseball game at Yankee Stadium. The first Yankee up smacked a single and the entire crowd stood up and shouted, "Run! Run!" as the runner streaked for first base.

The second batter hit a double and as the runners ran, the crowd, now including McTavish, again rose and shouted, "Run, man! Run!"

With men on second and third base, the pitcher walked the next man, throwing four balls out of the strike zone. The batter dropped his bat and strode to first base. McTavish rose and shouted, "Run, man! Run!"

His cousin pulled McTavish down and explained, "He doesn't have to run. He got four balls."

McTavish rose and shouted, "Walk with pride, man! Walk with pride!"

51. Tennis Thumb

[Toss this one off quickly.]

Tennis. Mixed doubles. Boomer Jones, a powerful player, sends a forehand rocket that just skims the net and smacks George, his net-playing male opponent, just below his belt. George sinks to the ground and doubles up in pain. His partner streaks over, says, "I'm an emergency room nurse and I know just what to do!" That said, she unsnaps his shorts, inserts her hand and starts massaging his private parts. After a few minutes, she asks, "Does that feel good?"

"Yes," he says. "<u>But my thumb still hurts.</u>"

52. Drag Harry

[Another one to toss off quickly.]

Charlie Schwartz goes off in the morning to play a round of golf with his buddies and doesn't get home tillafter dark. His wife is frantic. "What kept you so long?" she demands.

Charlie sinks into a chair in the living room, closes his eyes and sighs, "It was Harry. He collapsed and died on the third green. We didn't have a golf cart so we had to finish putting, tee up and take our strokes, drag Harry down the fairway, take a five iron to the green, drag Harry, putt, drag Harry...."

53. Mulligan

[When a golfer mis-hits a ball, he sometimes takes a stroke on his scorecard, tees up another ball and takes another shot. This is called a Mulligan.]

The police are called out to the golf club and find a golfer dead on the fairway with two deep dents in his head. A distraught golfer stands nearby. The investigating officer asks what happened.

"I shanked the ball and it hit him right in the head," the golfer explains.

"But how come there are two dents in his head?" the officer wants to know.

"I took a mulligan."

54. Golf Glasses

Arnold comes in off the golf course, angrily tosses his clubs in the corner of the locker room and mutters darkly about never playing again. His locker-neighbor, Sam, smiles, puts his hand on Arnold's shoulder and asks, "What's the matter?"

"What's the matter? Hooks, slices, shanks…that's what's the matter!" Arnold exclaims. "It's a crazy game."

"Not for me. Not since I got these golf glasses."

"Golf glasses?"

"Yup!" Sam removes his eyeglasses and hands them to Arnold. "These are made especially for golfers. When you look down, you'll see a large club and a small ball. When you look down the fairway, you'll see in the middle of the green a large hole. All you do is hit the small ball with the large club in the direction of the large hole. Try them! Go out again; play three holes!"

Arnold puts the glasses on, retrieves his clubs and exits. A half-hour later, he returns, exultant! "Unbelievable!" he shouts. "I did the first three holes in par!"

But Sam notices that Arnold's trousers are soaking wet around the crotch. Pointing, he asks, "What did I tell you! But…what happened?"

"Oh," Arnold says. "I got so excited, I couldn't stop playing and when I got back to the locker room, I really had to go. So without taking the glasses off, I opened my fly and took it out. And there were two of them, a big one and a small one. I didn't think the big one was mine, so I tucked it back inside...."

55. Golf Frog

"I take the day off from work and decide to go out golfing. I am on the fairway when I notice a frog sitting nearby. I think nothing of it and am about to shoot when I hear, 'Ribbit 9 iron.' I look around and don't see anyone. Again, I hear, 'Ribbit 9 iron.'

"I look at the frog and decide to prove the frog wrong, put the club away, and grab a 9 iron. Boom! I hit it 10 inches from the cup.

"I am shocked. I say to the frog, "Wow that's amazing! You must be a lucky frog, eh?" The frog replies, 'Ribbit lucky frog.'

"So I decide to take the frog to the next hole. 'What do you think, frog?' I ask.

"Ribbit 3 wood.

"I take out a 3 wood and, boom! Hole in one! I am befuddled and don't know what to say. By the end of the day, I have golfed the best game of golf in my life, and I ask the frog, 'OK where to next?'

"The frog replies, 'Ribbit Las Vegas.'

"So we go to Las Vegas and I say, "OK frog, now what?"

"The frog says, 'Ribbit roulette.'

"Se go to the roulette table and I ask, 'What do you think I should bet?'

"The frog replies, 'Ribbit $3000, black 6.'

"Now, this is a million-to-one shot to win, but after the golf game, I figure, What the heck? Boom! Tons of cash come sliding back across the table. I take my winnings and take the best room in the hotel. I sit the frog down and say, 'Frog, I don't know how to repay you. You've won me all this money and I am forever grateful.'

"The frog replies, 'Ribbit kiss me.' I figure why not, after all the frog did for me. With a kiss, the frog turns into a gorgeous 15-year-old girl. <u>And that, your honor, is how the girl ended up in my room.</u>"

56. Left-handed

[Introduction—The Best Part of Golf is the Jokes. For example….]

Couple's been married a number of years and they're out playing golf. As they walk down the fairway she says, "Harry…if anything…happened to me…would you marry again?"

After the briefest pause, he says, "Sure. I like being married."

"Oh." After some minutes, she adds, "But you wouldn't want to live in our house, the house we designed and built from scratch."

"Why not?" he replies, examining the head of his number 1 Driver. "It's a good, solid house. Good location."

"Oh." Some minutes later, she asks, "But you wouldn't…sleep in our bed."

"Sure I would!" he says, replacing the driver in his bag. "It's a good, solid bed with almost-new mattresses."

"Oh." As they approach the green, <u>she says in a voice grown husky,</u> "You wouldn't let her use my golf clubs, would you?"

<u>"No," he admits. "She's left-handed."</u>

BARS

[There are hundreds of bar jokes. You can use a somewhat silly one to set up your audience:]

57. Horse at the Bar

A guy is at the bar, nursing a drink, when a horse trots in, orders a martini, drinks it, pays and leaves. The guy, dumbfounded, points at the departing horse and croaks at the bartender: "Horse! That was a horse! A horse drank a martini!"

The bartender says in a soothing voice, "Calm down, now. It's unusual, I know it's unusual. That horse usually drinks rum swizzles."

[Now give them this one, which is best told after a few drinks.]

58. Monkey Balls

A fellow ordered a martini at a piano bar and watched a monkey scampering up and down the bar, munching peanuts and chattering. When the martini came, the monkey shot over, planted himself above the drink and dipped his balls into it.

The fellow, furious, demanded that the bartender get rid of the animal. The bartender, nonchalantly, told him that the monkey belonged to the piano player and he should talk to him.

Staring into the piano-player's rheumy, bloodshot eyes, the fellow snapped, "Do you know your monkey just dipped his balls in my martini?"

The piano player screwed up his face, shook his head and replied, "No, but hum a few bars and I'll fake it."

59. Tiger with Toothache

[Party joke. Put yourself <u>into</u> it! When the bartender roars, you roar; when the drunk whines, you whine.]

An alcoholic maneuvered his way up to a bar and demanded a drink.

"Get out of here, you bum!" the bartender roared. "You've cadged your last drink in this place. Go on, get!"

But the inebriate didn't budge. "I need a drink!" he whined.

The bartender leaned over and said, "You want a drink? I'll give you a drink. But you've got to do three things. I'll give you a whole bottle of vodka, but you've got to down it in five minutes. Then…you see those two doors?" pointing to two doors at the rear of the bar. "Behind the one on the left, chained to the wall, is a Siberian tiger with a toothache; take these pliers and pull the tooth. Then open the door on the right. You'll find Norma the nympho; no one's ever satisfied her. You do that, and you'll have free drinks here for life."

"Free drinks…for life," the alcoholic echos. The bartender breaks open a fifth of vodka and places it in front of the wino, who ups it and gurgles the whole bottle down in less than five minutes.

The bartender, surprised, hands him the pliers and points to the left door. The wino lurches to the rear of the bar, opens the door, and vanishes inside as the door swings shut. What follows is a terrifying chorus of roaring and shouting, banging and thudding until some ten minutes later, the door swings open and the fellow emerges, all bloody, with his clothes torn and his trousers hanging down around his knees. He makes his way to the bar and, waving the pliers, manages to stutter, "O…okay…now…where's the…girl with…the…toothache?"

60. Hickory Daiquiri

[This is a tame, clean joke fit for any group. Pronounce the drink—daiquiri—as: <u>dah-koree.</u>]

A dentist worked hard on his feet all day and liked to decompress on the way home by stopping in a certain bar for a certain drink: a daquiri, with crushed walnuts on top. He was so reliable and punctual that the bartender prepared the drink in advance so he wouldn't have to wait.

One afternoon, the bartender started to prepare the drink when he found himself out of crushed walnuts. So he substituted crushed hickory nuts. The dentist came in, took one sip and said, "This isn't my usual."

The bartender said, "No, <u>this is a hickory daquiri, doc!</u>"

BUSINESS

61. Refrigerator

[To be told at a fast pace.]

A travelling salesman returned a day early to his apartment in a high-rise to find a definite aroma of cigar in the air and his wife speechless in her sexiest negligee.

"Where is he? I'll kill him!" the salesman roared, and he frantically searched the closets, under the bed, behind the drapes....

Happening to glance out the kitchen window, which overlooked the front of the apartment, he spotted a man throwing on a jacket as he rushed out. "Aha!" and the salesman grabbed the first thing in his reach, which happened to be the refrigerator, and with an enormous burst of energy, heaved it out the window. A spasm of pain crossed his chest and he collapsed.

A short time later, at the gates of heaven, St. Peter saw a figure approaching. "Who are you and how did you get here?" St. Peter asked.

"I...I threw a refrigerator out my kitchen window and felt a great pain across my chest," the figure replied. "Next thing I know, here I am."

"Okay. Go into the waiting room while your case is judged."

A moment later, another figure shows up at the gates. "Who are you and how did you get here?" St. Peter asks.

"I was late for work and looking for a taxi and suddenly I see a shadow. I look up and there's this refrigerator coming down on top of me. That's all I know."

"Okay. Go into the waiting room while your case is worked on."

Minutes later, another figure approaches the gates.

"Who are you and how did you get here?"

Shaking his head, the person replies, "All I know is I was hiding in this refrigerator...."

62. Main Entrance

[Best told as an ethnic joke, with a slight accent. Have those signs clear in your mind as you start so you don't have to pause.]

For years, Cohen and Finkelstein—Hardware has prospered in the center of a block in downtown Brooklyn. Suddenly a big chain opens a store to the right, and a month later, another chain opens an outlet to the left. The chains put signs in their windows: BEST SELECTION...LOWEST PRICES...FREE DELIVERY...SENIOR DISCOUNT...SALE! SALE!

With business starting to fall off, Finkelstein wrings his hands and shakes his head. "What are we going to do?"

Cohen smiles. "They have so many signs in the windows you can't see the merchandise. So...."

Using a stencil on a piece of oaktag, he prints out a large sign and puts it over the door:

>>> MAIN ENTRANCE <<<

63. Fly Fishing

For whatever reason, Aberdeen and Finch, purveyors of sporting goods, have never hired a Jewish salesman, but with their main season approaching and finding themselves shorthanded, they hire Sam Schwartz. After a month, the receipts show that, though new to the business, Schwartz is outselling all their other salesmen by two to one! Aberdeen decides to investigate, so he comes down to the sales floor and hides behind a pile of merchandise. Soon a man enters the store and wanders over to Schwartz's station. A half-hour later, the man starts toward the street, laden with merchandise for fly-fishing; he's carrying everything from hip boots and fly-rods to a hat festooned with trout flies. Aberdeen intercepts him and asks, "Were you satisfied with our service? How about the salesman?"

"Oh, the service was excellent," the man says, "and your salesman...terrific."

"You do a lot of fly-fishing?"

"Never tried it, but I'm looking forward to a great experience."

"I'm sure you won't be disappointed. You did the right thing, coming to Aberdeen and Finch for your equipment."

"Oh, I didn't exactly come here for fly-fishing equipment. I came in to ask your salesman where the nearest drug-store was. My wife sent me out for a box of tampons. Mr. Schwartz told me it's only two blocks away, but added, 'As long as you're not going to be busy this weekend, why not try fly-fishing?' The canoe and the tent are being sent by United Parcel."

64. Two Elephants

[This must be told at a frantic pace, the punch line delivered slower and with a knowing smile.]

Sam encounters Lew on the street and grabs his shoulders. "Have I got a bargain for you! I'm gonna sell you something that's gonna change your life! I'm gonna sell you an elephant!"

"An elephant!" Lew retorts. "What am I gonna do with an elephant? I live in a three story two-bedroom walkup with a wife and four kids. Where am I gonna keep an elephant?"

"In the living room! But the best part is, this elephant is only gonna cost you two hundred bucks!"

"Two hundred bucks! I take home ninety dollars a week after taxes. I'm two months back on rent and we owe everyone in town! Where am I going to get two hundred dollars?"

"Lew, I'll tell you what I'm gonna do. I'm gonna sell you two elephants for only three hundred!"

Lew smiles. "Now you're talking business!"

DEFINITIONS

65. [This is like a shoehorn, slipped into a brief pause in conversation <u>where appropriate!</u> It's an entree to a longer story, which you should have ready.]

Mistress: What comes between a mister and a mattress.

66. [This story builds up as you tell it. Pause after '…and he proceeds…' and stress '<u>he</u>' has savoir-faire and don't be afraid to wave your finger knowingly in the air.]

Savoir-faire:

Three Frenchmen are seated at a table at an outdoor cafe in Montparnasse, trying to explain the meaning of 'savoir-faire' to an American. The first Frenchman says, "It is like this: If you come home from work to find your wife in bed with another man, and you close the door and go for a walk, you have savoir-faire."

"Non," says the second. "If you come home from work to find your wife in bed with another man and you say, 'Proceed', <u>then</u> you have savoir-faire."

"Not quite," says the third Frenchman. "If you come home from work to find your wife in bed with another man, and you say 'Proceed', <u>and he proceeds!</u>…then <u>he</u> has savoir-faire."

67. What is the difference between a viola and a violin?
    Answer: A viola burns longer.

DOCTORS

68. Ice the Elbow

A fellow's elbow is very painful and getting worse so he goes to the doctor, who suggests he ice it for ten minutes four times a day. He goes home and starts this but the pain is getting worse. The next day, the woman who comes in to clean the house sees him sitting in front of the TV with an icepack.

He explains his situation and she shakes her head. "Whenever I have an elbow problem, I put on a hot compress for a half-hour and that takes care of it."

The fellow exchanges his icepack for a hot compress and sure enough, by evening his pain is entirely gone! The next day he telephones his doctor. "I just want you to know that your icepacks didn't help at all and my cleaning woman with a sixth-grade education told me to try a hot compress and the pain is completely gone!"

"That's interesting," the doctor replied. "My cleaning woman advised me to use icepacks."

69. Stop Flogging

[The following is rated PG but you can segue into it with the right audience.]

Well, the hot compresses didn't solve the problem after all, and the fellow decided to see a big specialist with a reputation in diagnosis.

After waiting for an hour, he's told by the nurse to provide a urine specimen. Unfortun-ately, he'd just relieved himself and can't produce.

"Look, it's just an elbow problem," he implores. "What does a urine specimen have to do with it?"

But she's adamant—no specimen, no visit. He's to come back tomorrow.

He goes home and, suffering mightily, gets angrier by the hour. He produces a specimen…and then decides to add some of his wife's urine, and some of his daughter's and finally and for good measure, he gets some from the family dog.

The next day, he arrives at the doctor's office and hands over the specimen to the doctor, who opens the vial and sniffs its contents. Then, to make sure, he sniffs again. He puts the vial down and says,

"Your wife has gonorrhea. Your daughter's pregnant. Your dog has rabies. And if you don't stop flogging yourself, you're elbow's going to go out."

70. Ear Problem

[Tell at a brisk pace. Practice it so you don't laugh at the punch line.]

Fellow goes into a doctor's office, up to the nurse's station and asks to see the doctor.

"What's the problem?" she asks.

"Something's wrong with my penis," he says, rather loudly.

"Please!" she remonstrates sharply. "I have a waiting room full of patients here—they all don't have to hear such a graphic description of your problem! Use another word. Now go outside and come back in and start over."

He exits, re-enters, goes up to the nurse's station and asks to see the doctor.

"What's the matter?" the nurse asks, smiling.

"It's my ear," he says.

"What's the problem with it?" she asks.

He explains, "I can't pee out of it."

71. Strict Diet

A fellow has a mysterious illness and submits to a battery of tests so demanding he is put under complete sedation. When he wakes, he finds himself in bed in a completely white room. There is a bell on a tray, which he rings. His doctor's voice comes over an intercom.

"Ah. I see you're awake. We're still analyzing your test results; until we're certain your illness isn't contagious, we've put you in an isolation room, with a diet of flounder and pancakes."

"Why flounder and pancakes?" he asks.

"They're the only things that will fit under the door."

72. Tooth Extraction

A man is consulting with a dentist regarding a tooth extraction.

"Well, a proper extraction, with full anesthesia, will cost five hundred dollars," the dentist explains, "and there'll be no pain then or after."

"That's a bit high," the man says. "Can't it be done cheaper?"

"Well, I can give a local anesthetic. There'll be no pain during, but some discomfort afterward. That'll cost 250 dollars."

"Still high," the man sighs. "Is there a way to do it cheaper?"

"Well, I can give a topical. There'll be some pain during the procedure, and considerable discomfort for a week after. That'll cost fifty dollars."

"Fine," the man says, smiling. "I'll make an appointment for my wife."

73. Insurance

An older Jewish man is on the operating table awaiting surgery. At his insistence, his son, an experienced surgeon, is going to perform the operation. Just before they start the anesthesia, he asks to speak to his son.

"Yes, dad—what is it?"

"Don't be nervous. Do your best and just remember…if it doesn't go well—if something happens to me—your mother is going to come and live with you and your wife."

EUROPE

74. Noodles

[This is a classic Jewish story that could be taking place in a long-vanished, pre-World War II Poland. Make sure you have the lines down before starting.]

Perchickle would like to get married but doesn't know any girls and is rather afraid of them anyway, so he goes to a matchmaker.

"Women are just like men, my boy," the matchmaker said with his arm around the skinny <u>yeshiva bucher</u>* "They eat, so talk to them about food. They don't grow under bushes; they have family. So talk about family. And if you want to show what you're made of, talk about philosophy.

"I have a lady in my parlor right now; I'm going to introduce you and leave you alone to see how easy it is."

With that, he guides Perchickle into his parlor and there, sitting on a sofa, is a woman. A woman? Her forearms are nearly as thick as Perchickle's thighs and there are no smile lines on that stern countenance! A Valkyrie! All she needs is the winged helmet. Pushing his would-be suitor down beside her, the matchmaker makes introductions and vanishes.

Perchickle, suddenly perspiring, racks his brain. God help me! <u>Food</u>. Food! Looking up at the giantess, he asks meekly, "<u>Do you like noodles?</u>"

"I hate noodles!" she snaps.

His heart is fluttering. He'd get up and run, but fears his legs would fold and betray him. <u>Family</u>! Family! "How's your brother?" he ventures in a tiny voice.

"I don't have a brother!" she declares, her voice rattling the windows.

<u>Oh, G-d, wherefore hast Thou forsaken me!</u> Perchickle has one last chance. Philosophy. A statement. One sentence to show this woman what he had upstairs.

"<u>If…if you had a brother, do you think he'd like noodles?</u>"

* One who spends all his time in the <u>Yeshiva</u>, studying the Talmud.

75. Crazy Woman

[Here's an example of a double-header. If the preceding story went over well, follow up with this one.]

Pincus is also a <u>yeshiva bucher</u>, but unlike Perchick, he's thinks very highly of his qualifications as a prospective husband, though he has no money at all and hasn't worked a day in his life. He goes to a marriage broker and demands to see photographs of all the broker's clients. The broker shows him more than three dozen photographs, and Pincus dismisses every one. This one's too big; that one's too thin; the other has ears that stick out, etc. Finally the broker throws up his hands and says, "That's all, then."

But Pincus noticed one photograph placed backwards at the end of the album. "What about that one?" he asks. "Is she too homely to show?"

"On the contrary, she's the most beautiful girl I've ever represented."

"Oh. Then she has no dowry."

"Wrong again. Her father manages two of the Rothschilds operations. Her dowry equals all the others put together."

"Hm." Pincus touches his forehead. "Simple?"

"College degree from the Sorbonne. Speaks three languages but I won't waste any more of your time. There is a problem. Every year, for one day, she goes completely crazy. Stark, raving crazy. Incurable."

"One day a year!" Pincus exclaims. "I can live with that. Make the arrangements!"

"Not so fast," the broker sighs, regarding the impecunious student. "We'll have to wait for that day."

76. Only Child

[This joke requires a slight British accent for the Englishman's lines. Don't overdo it. A slight pause before the punch line, which is delivered rather coldly.]

An American businessman finds himself at an English resort hotel on a Sunday with nothing much to do. Venturing into the Clubroom, he finds an Englishman sitting there reading his London Times. Dropping down next to the formally-attired Englishman, the American introduces himself and asks whether they might play a few holes of golf.

"Tried it once; didn't like it," the Englishman says gruffly, returning to his paper.

"Some tennis, maybe," the American suggests.

"Tried it once; didn't like it," the Englishman snorts, rattling his newspaper.

"Bridge? I'm sure I can round up two more."

"Tried it once; didn't like it," the Englishman snaps.

"Billiards?"

"Tried it once; didn't like it! But 'ere comes my son; maybe he'd oblige you."

"Your only child, I presume."

77. Thought She Was British

[This one naturally follows the previous and requires no accent.]

During the Second World War, an American G.I. is brought into court in London immediately following an air raid. He was discovered during the raid having sex with a deceased female.

"How disgusting!" the magistrate thunders. "This is the worst example of necrophilia I have ever encountered! Have you anything to say for yourself?"

"I…I had no idea she was deceased, your Honor. I thought she was British."

78. Pissing in France

[This is a story with options; the short form or the long form, which requires some memorization and High School French. In my opinion, it is the funniest story in the collection. A slight French accent will give it flavor; singing the excerpt from The Marseillaise will bring down the house.]

{Short form}

A French farmer, a big, earthy fellow, is in a pissoire in Paris and next to him is a Parisian. The Parisian, glancing at his neighbor's penis, says, "I see you have the letters VE tattooed on your penis. Does that stand for Victory in Europe, a memorial to the end of the second world war?"

The farmer smiles. "Non, my friend. When we get…excited, it expands to read VERONIQUE! Ah, Veronique…."

Then, glancing down at the Parisian's penis, he notes the letters AE. "Aha!" he exclaims. "Let me guess. ALICE. Eh?"

"Non," the Parisian says, modestly. "When we get excited, it reads: 'Allons, enfents de la patrie, Le jour de gloire est arrive!'"

{Long Form—requires some French.}

A French farmer, a big, earthy fellow, is in a pissoire in Paris and to his right are two Parisians, both shorter and skinnier than he; the one farthest away looks positively scrawny, haggard. The Parisian next to him, glancing at the farmer's penis, says, "I see you have the letters VE tattooed on your penis. Is that a memorial to the end of the second world war?"

The farmer smiles. "Non, my friend. When we get...excited, it expands to read VERONIQUE! Ah, Veronique...."

Then, glancing down at the Parisian's penis, he notes the letters AE. "Aha!" he exclaims. "Let me guess. ALICE. Eh?"

"Non," the Parisian says, modestly. "When we get excited, it reads: 'Allons, enfents de la patrie, Le jour de gloire est arrive!'"

Both men laugh, then quiet down when they realize the other Parisian is urinating with the greatest difficulty. And on his penis is tattooed SE. The farmer asks, with sympathy, "The SE...it stands for...Salome?"

[The response is given in short, pained bursts.]

"Non, monsieur. It is...Souvenir...de la premier expedition...en Afrique...de la Legion Etrangier...de la Republique Francaise." (Souvenir of the first African expedition of the French Foreign Legion.)

79. The Bellringer

[This is a double-barrelled story that must be told with the right pacing—not too fast, not too slow. Pause after the first part.]

In a small village in Central Europe there was a church with a belltower. The bell was rung once each day at noon. When the clapper broke off and there was no money to buy another, they hired a man who volunteered to leap at the bell and strike it with his head. He would then grab the railing and save himself from falling to the ground. This went on okay until one day, he missed the railing and fell all the way down to the village square and was killed.

So badly mangled was he that they had to call the mayor to identify him. After a good look, the mayor said, "Well, I don't know his name but his <u>face rings a bell</u>."

*　　　　　*　　　　　*

(pause)

Fortunately they were able to replace him, and the new bellringer used the same technique as his predecessor…until the day when he, too, missed the railing and fell to the square. Again the mayor was called to identify him. After a careful look, the mayor said, "Well, I don't know his name but he's a <u>dead ringer</u> for our last fellow."

80. Holmes/Watson

[This (with some embellishment) is the top story in the world-wide contest run from the University of Hertfordshire, in Britain.]

Sherlock Holmes and Dr. Watson have gone camping. Pitching their tent under the open sky, they have gone to sleep. In the middle of the night, Holmes wakes Watson and says: "Watson, look up and tell me what you deduce!"

Watson says, "I see God's handiwork! The Moon! Millions of stars! Even if just a fraction of them have planets like Earth, surely there must be life out there! What are your thoughts, Holmes?"

"Watson, you idiot! It means that someone has stolen our tent!"

FANTASY

81. Prince Frog

[Straight delivery. At the punch line, look perplexed.]

A princess, walking alone in the woods, sat down to rest. A frog hopped up and croaked, "I'm not really a frog; I'm a prince changed into a frog by an evil witch. I'm doomed to remain a frog unless I spend the night on the pillow of a true princess."

Grinning, she said, "Froggie, it's your lucky day! I am a true princess and I will take you home with me. Just hide in my pocket."

That night, she put the frog on her pillow and sure enough, next morning, when she woke, she found a handsome, young prince in bed beside her.

But to this day, her mother doesn't believe that story.

82. Chastity Belt

[To be told with relish, at a good pace. Act out the punch line. If convenient, have a set of keys in your hand and mutter as if to yourself, "Now which one is it?" Professional comedians set a foundation with a strong joke, then build on it!]

Sir Galahad, about to leave for the crusades, calls his best friend, Sir Gawain, to his side. "I will be gone for at least two years, perhaps three at most. I have, of course, put a chastity belt on my wife that she not succumb to temptation in my absence. Should I not return after three years, you must assume that my body rests in the soil of Arabia and my soul is in heaven. Release my wife from her discomfort; here—I give you the key to her belt."

With that, Sir Galahad mounts his horse and, with his entourage, starts on the road to Jerusalem. They travel slowly and scarcely twenty minutes have passed before there is a cloud of dust in the road behind them and Sir Gawain pulls up, his horse panting. "Sir Galahad," Gawain cries, waving something in his hand. "<u>You gave me the wrong key</u>!"

83. Genie

[For ****, put in your own 'fall guy'.]

Following the sinking of their sailboat, three men—a Frenchman, an Italian and a **** are stranded on a desert island. Months pass; they live on a diet of coconut meat and milk, crabs and fish. One day a bottle washes up on shore and when they open it, a genie emerges. Tired after two thousand years in the bottle, the genie agrees to one wish each. The Frenchman weeps and asks only to be transported back to his home in Paris, where his family must be frantic with worry.

<u>Whoosh!</u> and he is gone.

The Italian, overcome with emotion, asks only to be returned to Venice, to his family and people.

<u>Whoosh!</u> and he is gone.

The ****, looking around, feels abandoned and says, "You know, it's lonely here without my friends. I wish they were back."

<u>Whoosh! Whoosh!</u>

84. The King's Jester

[Straight delivery. Pause very briefly before the punch line; don't give the listener a chance to guess it.]

The king's jester was fond of puns, and they kept getting worse and worse until one day the king ordered him to cease punning. Another one slipped out and the king had the jester thrown in the dungeon. The next morning, the jailor put a hood over his head and led him out to the courtyard, where a scaffold had been erected. He was led, weeping and wailing, up the steps; a rope was slipped over his head and the executioner awaited only the signal from the king to kick the trapdoor open.

The queen gave her husband a nudge in the side and whispered, "Now you've gone far enough! He was only trying to amuse you. Stop this right now!"

The king rose and announced, "I grant you a pardon on condition that you never tell another pun!"

The executioner removed the rope and the hood. The jester looked around and quipped, "No noose is good news."

<u>And they hung him.</u>

85. Onions

[The problem with this story is that it's difficult to conceal the punch line; that's why the diamond diversion is important. Don't slow down.]

There was once a kingdom that was rather isolated by high mountains and was ruled over by a genial king. He and the entire population loved to dine well and they spared no expense when it came to preparing food. A traveller came upon this place and found that, for all their emphasis on food, they had never heard of onions!

Returning to his native land, he purchased a cart and horse, loaded the cart with <u>baskets full of onions</u> and travelled through forests and over high passes until he'd returned to the kingdom. He was granted an audience with the king and announced that he'd brought something from his native land that would enhance the flavor of their foods tenfold.

The king said, "Tonight you will dine at the royal table and we will try it with a venison stew and if it's all you say, you will be richly rewarded. But if it's not...."

That evening they dined and the onions added such flavor, such richness to the stew that the king was overcome with delight. "You have said that you must leave tomorrow; you will find your cart full of the most precious possession in the kingdom."

The next morning, the traveller was delighted to find that his cart had been filled with silver bars. After expressing his gratitude to the king, he made his way over the mountain passes, through the forests and to his native land, where he made no secret of his success.

A countryman of his figured that if that wealthy king had given this fellow silver for onions, he'd probably give equal measure of gold...for garlic! So he bought a horse and cart, loaded it with baskets of garlic and made his way across mountain passes and through forests until he came to that kingdom. Introducing himself to the king, he announced that he'd brought a cart full of an herb that would improve the flavor of their food, not tenfold, but a hundredfold!

The king smiled and said, "Tonight you will dine at the royal table and we will try it with a beef stew and if it's all you say, you will be richly rewarded. But if it's not...."

The stew was all that the traveller had promised and the king was delighted. That night the traveller dreamed of gold, rubies, diamonds! The next morning, he said that he had to leave and was told that his cart was full of the most precious possession in the kingdom. He ran out and uncovered the cart...to find that it was filled with onions.

THE GOLDEN YEARS

86. Big Boys

[Quick joke. Straight delivery.]

A small boy is sitting on the curb, crying and watching older boys playing stickball in the street. An old man comes along and asks, "Why are you crying?"

"Because I can't do what the big boys do," the child snivelled.

The old man sat down and cried, too.

87. Wake at Seven

[Straight delivery. Pause before the punch line.]

Three golden-agers are comparing their early-morning problems.

"I get up in the morning, and go into the bathroom and stand there, and stand there maybe for ten minutes and finally I get a dribble," says Max.

"Hah!" says Sidney. "I run the water in the sink, and think about Niagara Falls and maybe after fifteen minutes something comes out."

Louis says, somewhat proudly, "With me, it's not so bad. Every morning at six-thirty, whoosh! it comes, like clockwork. The only problem is…I first wake up at seven."

88. Pinwheel Smith

[Straight delivery. A quickie.]

Geraldine Smith passes away at a ripe age with a smile on her face and, on reaching the Pearly Gates, asks to be reunited with her late husband.

"What was his name?" St. Peter asks as he checks her earthly record.

"John Smith."

"Do you realize how many John Smiths we have up here?" St. Peter says. "Did he have any outstanding characteristics? Did he win any major prizes? Give generously to charity? Anything?"

Geraldine shakes her head.

"Well, what were the last words he said before he passed on?"

"Oh. He told me that if I were ever unfaithful to his memory, he'd turn over in his grave."

"Aha!" St. Peter says. "You want 'Pinwheel' Smith!"

89. Miami Beach

[Straight delivery. Deliver the punch line wistfully.]

Two octogenarian women are walking along the beach in Miami and they enter a section reserved for nudists. A man, lying on his back, has fallen asleep and the wind has gradually covered his body except for his nose and his penis, which is fully extended. One woman stares and says to her friend, "Look at that, Gertrude! When I was twenty, my mother warned me to stay away from that. When I was forty, I couldn't get enough of it. When I was sixty, I paid for it. And now that I'm eighty, it grows wild on the beaches in Miami!"

90. Old Man's Had It

[Straight delivery.]

An elderly man—stooped, four-pronged cane, trifocal glasses—goes into a brothel and tells the madam he'd like a young girl for the night. Surprised, she looks at him and asks how old he is.

"I'm ninety-three years old," he says.

"Ninety-three!" she snorts. "Don't you realize you've had it?"

"Oh, sorry," says the man. "How much do I owe you?"

91. Single

[The punch line must be delivered just right, with a honeyed voice, stressing the word <u>single</u>.]

A woman of uncertain years is seated on a park bench in Florida. A pale-faced man, neatly but inexpensively dressed and needing a shave and haircut, approaches. He drops onto the other end of the bench, closes his eyes and turns his face to the sun.

"You're new in this neighborhood, aren't you?" she asks.

"Yup."

"You haven't been in Florida long, have you?"

"Nope. Just got here."

"From where did you come, if you don't mind my asking?"

"Sing Sing."

"Sing Sing. I've heard of that."

"It's a prison. I've just got out, lady, after fifteen years."

"Oh, you poor man!" she exclaims. "What did you do?"

"I killed my wife."

After a few moments, she moves closer on the bench and says in a <u>honeyed voice</u>, "<u>So you're single</u>...!"

92. Drop Dead

Six retired Floridians are playing poker in the clubhouse when Meyer loses a hundred fifty dollars on a single hand, clutches his chest and drops dead at the table. The other five, out of respect to Meyer, continue playing standing up.

When it's time to quit, Finkelstein asks, "So who's going to tell the wife?"

They draw straws. Goldberg loses and, soberly, promises to handle this discretely, like a <u>mensch</u>. He goes to the Meyer apartment, knocks on the door. The wife answers and asks what he wants.

"Your husband just lost a hundred fifty dollars in poker and is afraid to come home."

"A hundred fifty dollars! Tell him he should drop dead!" she yells.

"I'll go tell him," says Goldberg.

93. One Word or Two

[Deliver the punch line clearly, thoughtfully, deliberately.]

An elderly couple had been dating for some time. Finally they decided to get married. Before the wedding, they went out to dinner and discussed how their marriage might work. Finances. Living arrangements and so on. Finally the old gentleman broached the subject of their physical relationship.

"How do you feel about sex?" he asked.

"Well," she responded, "I'd have to say I would like it infrequently."

The gentleman thought for a long moment, then asked, "Is that one word or two?"

94. Grandmas Driving

Sitting on the side of the highway waiting to catch speeding drivers, a State Police Officer sees a car puttering along at 22 MPH. He thinks to himself "This driver is just as dangerous as a speeder!" So he turns on his lights and pulls the driver over.

Approaching the car, he notices that there are five old ladies—two in the front seat and three in the back—wide eyed and white as ghosts. The driver, obviously confused, says to him, "Officer, I don't understand, I was doing exactly the speed limit! What seems to be the problem?"

"Ma'am," the officer replies, "You weren't speeding, but you should know that driving slower than the speed limit can also be a danger to other drivers."

"Slower than the speed limit? No sir, I was doing the speed limit exactly…Twenty two miles an hour!" the old woman says a bit proudly.

The State Police officer, trying to contain a chuckle explains to her that "22" was the route number, not the speed limit. A bit embarrassed, the woman grinned and thanked the officer for pointing out her error. "But before I let you go, Ma'am, I have to ask…Is everyone in this car ok? These women seem awfully shaken and they haven't muttered a single peep this whole time."

"Oh, they'll be alright in a minute officer. We just got off Route 90."

95. The Jar

An 85-year-old man went to his doctor's office to get a sperm count. The doctor gave the man a jar and said, "Take this jar home and bring back a semen sample tomorrow."

The next day the 85-year-old man reappeared at the doctor's office and sadly gave him the jar, which was as clean and empty as on the previous day. The doctor asked what happened and the man explained:

"Well, doc, it's like this—First I tried with my right hand. Nothing.

"Then I tried with my left hand, but still nothing. Then I asked my wife for help. She tried with her right hand, then her left, still nothing. She tried with her mouth, first with the teeth in, then with her teeth out, and still nothing. We even called up Arleen, the lady next door and she tried too, first with both hands, then an armpit and she even tried squeezin' it between her knees, but still nothing."

The doctor was shocked! "You asked your neighbor?"

The old man replied, "Yep. And no matter what we tried, we still couldn't get the jar open."

96. Forgot her Name

At a wedding dinner, there's one older couple at a table. Throughout the dinner, he addresses his wife as Darling, Honey, Sweetheart....

After she's left to go to the powder room, the woman sitting next to the older man leans over and says, "I think it's beautiful the way, after all your years together, you still call your wife Darling and Honey."

"Well," he admits, "frankly, I forgot her name five years ago."

97. The Baby Cries

By a miracle of medicine, Bertha Goldstein was able to conceive and carry a baby to term at the age of 62. A week after she'd brought the baby home, some of her friends dropped in to have a look at the miracle-child. Bertha sat them down in the living room and chatted about how wonderful it was to be a mother at her age...and chatted...and chatted...until one of the visitors asked if they could see the baby.

"Not yet," Bertha said, and continued talking.

After some more minutes, another woman asked if they could see the baby now.

"Not yet," Bertha said. "We have to wait until the baby cries."

"Why?" the woman demanded.

"I forgot where I left her," Bertha said.

98. Disability

An old man went into the Social Security Office and filled out an application.

He was too old to have a birth certificate, so he was asked to prove his age. He opened his shirt and showed them the grey hair on his chest. They accepted that as proof, and give him his first check.

He went home to his wife, showed her the check, and explained to her what had happened.

She replied, "Well get back down there, pull down your pants, and see if you can also get disability!"

99. Looking your Age

[This is tailor-made for a woman to relate. Introduce with this "confession":]

I have been guilty of looking at others my own age and thinking...surely I cannot look that old.........I'm sure you've done the same...

While waiting for my first appointment in the reception room of a new dentist, I noticed his certificate, which bore his full name. Suddenly, I remembered that a tall, handsome boy with the same name had been in my high school class some 40 years ago. Upon seeing him, however, I quickly discarded any such thought. This balding, gray-haired man with the deeply lined face was too old to have been my classmate. After he had examined my teeth, I asked him if he had attended the local high school.

"Yes," he replied.

"When did you graduate?" I asked.

He answered, "In 1957."

"Why, you were in my class!" I exclaimed.

He looked at me closely and then asked, "What did you teach?"

HEAVEN & HELL

[Jokes 1 and 2 form a natural double—as soon as the laughter (hopefully) subsides from joke 1, start joke 2.]

100. Hard

Three young women are driving, get into a terrible crash and find themselves at the gates of heaven. St. Peter, after checking their earthly records, explains, "Well, you came to the right place. It used to be that you just walked in, but now you have to answer a question first."

The women are upset and nervous, but St. Peter reassures them that this is just <u>pro forma</u>; that the questions aren't difficult. To the first woman, he asks, "Who was the first man?"

Relieved, she responds, "<u>That's easy—Adam</u>," and with a flourish of trumpets, the gates roll open. She enters heaven.

To the second woman, St. Peter asks, "Your question is:
Who was the first woman?"

"<u>That's easy! Eve!</u>" And once more the gates roll open and the woman hurries into heaven.

To the third woman, St. Peter asks, "Your question is: What were the first words Eve said to Adam?"

Anxiously scratching her head, she replies, "<u>Oh. That's hard</u>." [Pause two seconds!]

<u>And with a flurry of trumpets, the gates open</u>....

101. Virginia Pipelini

The same three woman, after rattling around heaven for a while, come back to St. Peter and ask for leave to visit Earth, just for a day. He reviews their records and grants them their wish, and allows them to take the persona of anyone they'd ever wished to be.

"Oh, wonderful!" exclaims the first. "I've always admired Gina Lollabrigida." With a wave of his hand, St. Peter sends her down, an exact clone of the famous actress.

"I'd love to be Eleanor Roosevelt, just for a day," the second woman says. No sooner wished than granted, and she's gone.

"I...I'd like to be Virginia Pippelini," the third woman whispers.

"Who?" St. Peter asks.

"Virginia Pippelini. Here. Read the headline." From the pocket of her robe she takes a newspaper clipping and gives it to St. Peter.

After glancing at it, he returns it, shaking his head. "You read it wrong. The headline reads: Virginia <u>Pipeline</u> laid by five hundred men in one day."

102. Communist Hell

[European humor tends to be political.]

A certain fellow passes on and his soul wakens to find itself in a white room with two doors, one labelled Capitalist Hell, the other Communist Hell. He isn't exactly surprised to find that he didn't make the cut to Heaven, and not knowing what to do, opens the door to Capitalist Hell and peeks inside.

A dreadful scene! Folks are lying on beds of nails, with imps pouring flaming oil over them and demons lashing them with whips! He closes the door...and suddenly a uniformed guide appears, with his dossier. "Well, well, well..." the guide says, looking over the dossier and nodding.

"You have your choice of hells. Capitalist or Communist. Take a look and decide."

The fellow opens the door to Communist Hell and sees the same scene; people lying on beds of nails, with flaming oil and whips. "Well, I already looked in the other place and I don't see a difference," he moans. "They're both very dreadful."

The guide nods, then whispers, "'You're not so bad a chap…take the Communist Hell. Sometimes they run out of nails, sometimes they can't ignite the oil and when the whips break, they don't get replaced immediately…."

103. Israeli Bus Driver

A bishop passes on and finds himself at the end of a long line of souls outside the gates to heaven. He's resigned to waiting when he sees another arrival bypass the line, pause briefly at the gates and march straight into the Eternal afterlife. Calling over a guide, he says, "There must be a mistake. I was a bishop of the church for many years. I preached the Word every morning and twice on Sundays. Why do I have to wait on line to get my reward when someone not of the cloth marches right into heaven?"

The guide thumbs through his registry, nods and explains, "It's true, you gave eight sermons each week and put most of the congregation to sleep. That man who just went in was an Israeli bus driver and by the way he handled his bus, he put the fear of God in more people in one trip than you accomplished in twenty years of sermons.

ISRAEL

104. Kibbutz Size

[Act this out, pointing to left and right as though you were the kibbutz manager. Try for a realistic Texas drawl when speaking his part.]

A group of Americans touring Israel are visiting a kibbutz, whose manager is very proud of the size of his kibbutz. Pointing to the left, he says, "You see that row of trees in the distance?" Then, to the right, "And over there, way over there is a steel shed. And straight ahead, almost three kilometers away you see a stone wall. That's how big this kibbutz is!"

One of the tourists is from Texas. He can't hold back. "Son," he says, "back home, I get up before dawn and make me a picnic lunch. Then I get in my car and drive as fast as the car will go in a straight line, until noon. That's when I stop and eat that lunch. Then I keep going until sunset, and that's when I reach the front gate of my ranch! What do you think of that?"

The Israeli nods and says, sympathetically, "Yeah, I used to have a car like that."

105. Shapiro the Spy

Johnnie Sullivan of the C.I.A. is summoned into his boss's office and handed a manila envelope, sealed and stamped OPERATION MOIL TURMOIL. "You're to fly to Israel, take precautions to make sure you're not being followed, then rent a car and go to 301 Mandelbaum—an apartment house—and give this to Shapiro. This is TOP SECRET—EYES ONLY. Memorize the knock and your lines. If you're compromised, press twice on the letters P and U; the envelope will burst into flame. This is your first overseas mission—good luck."

Sullivan flies El Al, arriving in the late morning. He checks in at his hotel, walks down the rear stairway to the street, takes standard precautions to ensure that he's not being followed, then rents a car and drives to 301 Mandelbaum. On the register in the antechamber, he sees that there are two Shapiros, one on the ground floor, one on the seventh. He presses the button for the ground floor Shapiro and is buzzed inside. He knocks on Shapiro's door according to his instructions—two raps, one, then three.

The door flies open. The apartment is dark. A skinny man wearing thick-lensed glasses blinks in the sudden light. "The grass grows green by the sea of Sighs," Sullivan recites, as per his instructions.

"Oh. I'm Shapiro the tailor," says the resident. "You want Shapiro the spy; he's on the seventh floor."

106. Dress in the Tuchus

[This doesn't have to be a Jewish joke. It could relate to any religious denomination.]

It's the Sabbath, and Morris Goldstein is getting ready to go to synagogue. "Are you coming, Becky?" he asks.

"Not today. My ankle hurts and besides it may rain. Go, and I'll have a nice lunch ready for later."

Morris goes, and returns at around one o'clock with a shiner on his right eye.

"My God, what happened?" Rebecca says as she applies a cold compress.

"It wasn't my fault," Morris groans. "I sat in our usual seat and in front of me, Sarah Schwartz. We came to the part of the service where everyone stands up and when Sarah stands, her dress is caught in the crack of her behind. I know how uncomfortable that is, so I reach over and pull it out and she turns around and gives me this <u>clop</u> right in the face!"

"Aha!" cries Rebecca. "How many times have I told you—keep out of other people's business! You're always interfering…." Rebecca gives him a good ten minutes worth of advice plus another ten that evening, for good measure.

A week passes, Morris's eye clears up and again it's the Sabbath. "Are you coming to shul, Becky?" he asks.

"Not today. My ankle still bothers me. You go, <u>and stick to your own business!</u>"

Morris leaves and returns at about one o'clock and this time it's his left eye that has the shiner. As soon as he walks in, he exclaims, "This time it wasn't my fault, not one bit!"

As his wife applies the cold compress, he explains, "I was walking to shul and I meet up with Jake Rabinowitz. We walk together, we sit together and Mrs. Schwartz in front. <u>Again</u>, we come to the part of the service where everyone stands and <u>again</u> her dress is caught in the crack of her behind. <u>Jake</u> leans forward and pulls it out! <u>I know she doesn't like that, so I reach forward and put it back in….</u>"

107. The Meat Shortage

A roving reporter stopped a Texan on a New York street and asked, "Excuse me, could you give me your opinion on the meat shortage?"

The Texan replied, "What meat shortage?"

Next, the reporter stopped a Russian and asked, "Excuse me, could you give me your opinion on the meat shortage?"

The Russian said, "What's a shortage?"

Moving on, the reporter stopped a Pole and asked, "Excuse me, could you give me your opinion on the meat shortage?"

The Pole replied, "What's meat?"

Finally the reporter stopped an Israeli and asked, "Excuse me, could you give me your opinion on the meat shortage?"

The Israeli asked, "What's Excuse me?"

108. Only the Lubavitchers

[The punch line should be delivered with a trace of an accent.]

The astronomers have detected the imminent arrival of a spacecraft from another world! Communication is no problem; the aliens have been studying our languages for years. The spacecraft will descend into Yankee Stadium. All the heads of state are present to meet the first aliens to ever make contact with Earthlings. The spacecraft descends and lands gently. An orchestra strikes up appropriate music as a panel unfolds and the first representative of another world strides down to meet the secretary-general of the United Nations.

The alien is tall, humanoid and attired in black from hat to shoes, including a long, black coat. He has a grey beard and tufts of grey hair dangling from the sides of his narrow face.

The secretary-general, astonished, asks, "Do all men from your planet dress like that?"

"No," comes the answer in a resonant voice. "Only the Lubavitchers."

109. Ribbon

[General Hint: To avoid confusion with names, partner the first letters with their corresponding roles. Rabinowitz sells Ribbon; Hermann sells Hats. Give Rabinowitz a slight European accent.]

Rabinowitz leaves Poland when it's a good thing to do and settles on the lower East Side of New York, where he eventually opens a store selling ribbons. He's in that store thirty-five years, and down the block is Hermann, also from Poland, selling hats.

Finally Rabinowitz decides to close his store and retire, but first he goes to Hermann and complains, "For thirty-five years we're on the same block doing business and you've never once bought ribbon from me!"

"I don't use much ribbon," Hermann says.

"So buy what you need! But never to buy even one foot of ribbon…it's a disgrace!"

Hermann thinks, then says, smiling, "Okay. I'll buy plain red ribbon. A half-inch wide, and long enough to reach from the tip of your nose to the tip of your penis."

"It's a deal!" Rabinowitz says.

The next day a trailor-truck pulls up in front of Hermann's store and men start unloading huge spools of red ribbon, twenty-thousand feet to the spool. Hermann runs to Rabinowitz's store and shouts, "What's going on? Your men are delivering miles of ribbon!"

"Of course," Rabinowitz says. "You said enough to reach from the tip of my nose to the tip of my shmeckle. The tip of my nose is here in New York. For sixty-five years, the tip of my shmeckle has been in Poland."

[Note: The punch word is <u>Poland;</u> it should be the last word for maximum effect. This is better wording than: "The tip of my shmeckle has been in Poland for sixty-five years."]

110. The Four Sons

Four Jewish brothers became doctors, manufacturers, Hedge Fund operators, whatever…they all prospered mightily. Chatting after a dinner, they discussed the gifts that they had been able to give to their elderly mother for the previous Chanukah. The first bragged, "I had a big house built for Mama."

The second, not to be outdone, said, "I had a hundred thousand dollar theater built in the house so she could see movies."

The third broke in, smirking, "I had my Mercedes dealer deliver her an SL600 with a chauffeur."

The fourth waved his hand, blowing all that away and announced, "Listen to this. You know how Mama loves reading the Torah and you know she can't see very well. I sent her a parrot that can recite the entire Torah. It took five rabbis 10 years to teach him. I had to pledge to contribute $50,000 a year for twenty years but it was worth it. Mama just has to name the chapter and verse and the parrot will recite it."

Soon thereafter, Mom sent out her Thank You notes. She wrote: "Milton, the house you built is so huge. I live in only one room, but I have to clean the whole house. But thanks so much."

"Menachem, you give me a theater with Dolby sound, it could hold 50 people, but all my friends are dead, I've lost my hearing and I'm nearly blind. Thanks anyway."

"Marvin, I am too old to travel. I stay home, I have my groceries delivered, so I never use the Mercedes…and the driver is a Nazi. But a million thanks."

"Dearest Melvin, you were the only son to have the good sense to give a little thought to your gift. The chicken was delicious."

LAWYERS

111. Lawyers for Rats

There are three reasons why testing laboratories these days are using lawyers more than rats.

1. There are more lawyers than rats and sometimes the supply houses run short of rats.

2. Sometimes one becomes attached to a lab rat.

3. There are some things a rat won't do.

112. I'll Screw...

A man walks into a bar and sees a beautiful, well-dressed woman sitting on a bar stool alone. He walks up to her and says, "Hi there, how's it going?"

She turns to him, looks him straight in the eyes and says, "I'll screw anybody, anywhere, your place or mine, it doesn't matter."

The guy raises his eyebrows and asks, "Really? What law firm do you work for?"

113. Divorce Lawyer

It's nearly the end of the 'happy hour' at Johnny's Bar and a slightly tipsy man, after telling a string of lawyer jokes, is preparing to amuse his fellow imbibers by doing a magic trick. Turning away from his audience, he inserts a few dimes in each nostril, intending to rain money as the punch line of a joke. But he pushes the coins up too far and suddenly finds he can't breathe.

He falls to the floor and starts turning blue as the bystanders and the barman try the Heimlich maneuver and CPR and every method of resuscitation they ever heard of. Suddenly a woman dashes into the crowd, elbows everyone aside, reaches down and unzips his fly. Reaching inside, she grabs his testicles and squeezes with all her strength.

The coins come flying out and soon the natural color is returning to the man's face.

"Wow!" exclaims one of the bystanders. "Are you an emergency physician?"

"No," she says. "I'm a divorce attorney."

114. Lawyer Joke-string

[Below is a string of quickies—tell no more than three at a time, but in rapid-fire.]

a) How can a pregnant woman tell that she's carrying a future lawyer?
   ** She has an uncontrollable craving for baloney.

b) How does an attorney sleep? ** First he lies on one side, then he lies on the other.

c) How many lawyer jokes are there? ** Only three. The rest of the stories are true.

d) How many lawyers does it take to change a light bulb? ** How many can you afford?

e) If a lawyer and an IRS agent were drowning and you could only save one of them, would you go to lunch or read the paper?

f) What do you call a lawyer with an I.Q. of 80? ** Your Honor.

g) What does a lawyer use for birth control? ** His personality.

h) Why does California have the most lawyers in the country and New Jersey the most toxic waste sites? ** New Jersey got first choice.

115. Professional Courtesy

[This is rather old, but it is a classic.]

Following the sinking of an overcrowded cruise ship, a handful of passengers find themselves in a lifeboat without oars. An island is not too far away, but without oars, the only way they'll get there is if one of them swims, pulling the boat. And in every direction one sees the fins of circling sharks.

"I can't do it," says one man. "I'm a surgeon, the only specialist in eye transplants in New York. I have operations lined up for two years; those people will go blind if I'm not there."

"I'd do it," says another. "But I'm a diplomat with the United Nations. Next Monday, we're going to try to arrange a truce between two Asian countries that are on the brink of war. If I'm not there to smooth things out, their representatives will be at each other's throats in no time. War will break out, and millions may die."

"I'll go," says the third man, and removing his outer clothing, he dives into the water, takes the rope and swims powerfully until, an hour later, he beaches the lifeboat. "But how come the sharks didn't go for you?" says the surgeon, astonished.

"I'm a lawyer. Professional courtesy."

116. Cigars

[This is probably the best lawyer story of the year. It is a true story and was the 1st place winner in a recent Criminal Lawyers Award Contest. However, one must get the legal language correct, or it loses its authenticity.]

A Charlotte, NC, lawyer purchased a box of <u>very rare and expensive cigars</u>, then <u>insured</u> them against fire among other things. Within a month, having smoked his entire stockpile of these great cigars and <u>without yet having made even his first premium payment on the policy</u>, the lawyer filed claim against the insurance company. In his claim, the lawyer stated the cigars were <u>lost "in a series of small fires</u>." The insurance company refused to pay, citing the obvious reason:

That the man had consumed the cigars in the normal fashion was obvious. The lawyer sued.... and won! In delivering the ruling the judge agreed with the insurance company that <u>the claim was frivolous</u>. The Judge stated <u>nevertheless</u>, that the lawyer held a policy from <u>the company</u> in which it <u>had warranted that the cigars were insurable and also guaranteed that it would insure them against fire, without defining what is considered to be unacceptable fire</u>," and was obligated to pay the claim. Rather than endure lengthy and costly appeal process, the insurance company <u>accepted the ruling and paid $15,000.00 to the lawyer for his loss of the rare cigars</u> lost in the "fires."

NOW FOR THE BEST PART...

After the lawyer cashed the check, the insurance company had him arrested on <u>24 counts of ARSON</u>!!!! With <u>his own insurance claim</u> and testimony from the previous case being <u>used against him</u>, the lawyer was convicted of intentionally burning his insured property and was sentenced to 24 months in jail and a $24,000.00 fine.

MARRIAGE

117. Tomorrow She Dies

[This is a classic. Build up the last scene with details on George's decrepitude.]

George goes to see his old college friend, Dr. Michael Addams, waits until the waiting room is clear, then is ushered into Michael's office. Closing the door, he talks in a low voice, explaining that he can no longer live with his wife and she won't give him a divorce. He has no choice—he's going to have to do her in. For old time's sake, he'd like to do it in a merciful...and untraceable...way. Is there a pill...a potion....?

"No way, George," Dr. Addams says, firmly. "The police labs are too good these days. You end up in jail and at the very least, I lose my license. The only thing...some doctors believe that if a woman has sex ten times a day, she can't last more than thirty days."

"Mike, you're an ace!" George exclaims, and with a wicked smirk on his face, he rushes out.

Twenty-nine days pass. Dr. Addams hasn't heard from George and decides to drop over at George's house on the way home. Cautiously he walks down the path past the kitchen, hears a noise from the back yard and pokes his head around the corner of the house. There, in the neighbor's back yard is a tennis court and George's wife is playing a hard game of singles, her long hair flying this way and that as she covers the court, whacking the ball into the corners and serving aces almost at will.

Dr. Adams retreats and finds himself outside the master bedroom. He peers inside…and there's George in bed. His friend's clawlike fingers grasp the cover; his eyes are sunk in a skull-like face. He cannot weigh more than ninety pounds.

Mike throws open the window and calls out, "George! George! Are you okay?"

George parts his lips in a cadaverous smile and whispers, "Yeah, Doc. And thanks. Little does she know that tomorrow she dies."

118. Honeymoon

[This is a double-barrelled joke. The first one isn't that funny, but it sets up the second.]

The ceremony is finally over and off they go to their honeymoon in the Poconos hotel, John and Gladys. John hasn't been around much; he was home-schooled by his mother, never went to summer camp, didn't have many friends and got married only because Gladys talked him into it.

That evening, Gladys, having perfumed herself, is waiting in bed. John is standing by the window, looking out at the night sky.

"Aren't you coming to bed?" she asks.

"Later," he replies. "My mother told me this would be the most beautiful night of my life and I don't want to miss a minute of it."

∗   ∗   ∗

John, having figured out what Gladys has in mind, undresses.

"Oh, what a cute pee-pee!" she says.

Taken aback, John says, "Now, Gladys, I know you ain't been around much, but the right name for this thing is…a dick."

"Oh," she exclaims. "That's not a dick. My friend George had a dick! Henry had a real shlong! And Marvin, he was hung like a horse! No, that's a pee-pee."

119. Lion's Wedding

The animals in the jungle were celebrating the lion's wedding. There was music and food and drink and the guest who was dancing with the greatest abandon was the mouse. During a pause, the turtle asked the mouse why he was celebrating so wildly.

"Because it is my brother who is getting married!" the mouse exclaimed.

"But you are a mouse!" the turtle said. "How can a lion be your brother?"

"Oh, before I was married, I was a lion also."

120. Love Suit

A recently-married girl lived not too far from her mother-in-law, who sometimes dropped over to visit. One day, toward evening, the mother-in-law rang the bell and was astonished to find her daughter-in-law open the front door, stark naked.

"Alice! What is this?" the mother-in-law cried.

"Oh, this is my love suit," the girl explained. "Arthur likes it when I greet him this way at the end of a long day at work. Now you'd better not stay; he'll be home any minute!"

The mother-in-law, leaving, thinks about this. Her husband will be home shortly from work. At home, she undresses and when she hears his car pull up, stands in the doorway, smiling and wearing only earrings. He opens the door and stands there, gaping.

"What's this?" he asks.

"I'm wearing my love suit," she says, coyly.

"Well, it needs a pressing."

121. What they All Paid

[This is a triple-header, each feeding the next.]

Jack Newman, a top-notch salesman in his late sixties, comes home from the doctor with devastating news. "One more road trip and I'm a goner!" he cries to his wife, Rebecca. "He tells me I can't take the pressure of sales any more; everything inside is shot! So how are we going to live? Welfare?"

"Heaven forbid!" Rebecca says. Then, squaring her shoulders, she says, "I will go out and earn money."

"How are you gonna do that?" he moans. "You have no training, no specialty."

"I'm a woman," she declares. "I will earn money by being a woman! I will start first thing in the morning."

And sure enough, right after breakfast, Rebecca, tarted up with broad slashes of lipstick, high heels and a slit down the side of a black skirt, leaves the apartment while her husband wrings his hands that it has come to this!

Noontime comes, then dinnertime and night falls and Jack doesn't hear from her. Frantic, he paces and listens to news programs, expecting to hear the worst. Ten o'clock, eleven o'clock...and finally, at nearly midnight, there is a key in the door and Rebecca stumbles into the foyer. Her hair is wild, her face smudged, her clothes wrinkled and she can barely walk, but triumphantly she overturns her purse and pours onto the dining-room table her profit.

"Ninety-three dollars and fifty cents," she croaks, sinking into a chair.

"Oh, my God!" Jack whispers. "But how come fifty cents? Where did that come from?"

"Oh, that's what they all paid!"

122. Mother's Milk

Jack's condition gets worse and now the doctor tells him that unless he gets fresh mother's milk every evening, he's a goner. Rebecca can't provide this, but dutifully, with her husband's life at stake, she makes a few phone calls and soon finds that there's a recent widow nearby who's just given birth and is breast-feeding her infant. Rebecca makes the arrangements, and wringing her hands, sees Jack off.

He arrives at the apartment to find that the woman is quite young, very attractive and the baby is sound asleep. She seats herself on her sofa, removes her blouse and nursing bra, and motions Jack to get started. He does and as he nurses, she feels urges that she hasn't felt since her husband died.

"Tell me," she asks tenderly during a pause, "is there anything else I can...do for you?"

"No," Jack says, resuming.

Her blood is warming up and there are powerful stirrings in her loins. "Are you sure there isn't something I can...do for you?" she asks, blushing.

"No, thanks," Jack says, switching to the other breast.

"There must be something...you'd like!" she cries.

Jack pulls away and, hesitating just for a moment, says, "<u>Maybe you got a cookie?</u>"

123. Motorcycle

Jack pulls through, is cured and inherits a few million from an uncle. He and Rebecca are in their seventies now, and on their fiftieth anniversary, to repay her for all she's done for him over the years, he's gotten her a present to end all presents. After breakfast, she says, "So how are we going to celebrate? A walk in Central Park and lunch in a fancy restaurant, maybe?"

Jack smiles. "Not quite, Becky! For you I got a surprise. Go look out the window and down."

She does. "All I see are people walking and horse-drawn carriages and…what's that in front of the apartment? Motorcycles! We have Hell's Angles in the building now?"

"That's Hell's Angels, Becky," Jack says. "And those motorcycles belong to the newest members. You and me."

"What!"

"Your's is the pink one with the bow. But first, look in the guest closet; there's a box with your proper Hell's Angels clothing. Black leather pants, a black jacket, a helmet…everything. Put them on; we're going for a cruise! But first, to get the feel of it, go sit on the motorcycle and get it started."

Laughing, Rebecca dresses in the outfit and while Jack is fussing with his appearance, she takes the elevator down to see what she can do about this. With the doorman's help, she climbs onto her machine, gets it started and sits there while the powerful engine throbs.

A cop comes along and, leaning over, tells her that she's in a no-parking zone and has to move the motorcycle.

"I can't," she says, bouncing up and down.

"Lady, you have to," he says, reaching for his ticket book.

Now her body is vibrating in harmony with the powerful machine. "I can't," she gasps and then she abandons herself to an internal explosion.

"Lady," he says….

"Officer," she interrupts, breathing heavily. "Kiss me, quick!"

124. That's One

A man and woman marry after a short but intense courtship and they honeymoon at the HeartFelt Dude Ranch. The morning after their arrival they sign up for a ride. She's given Daisy, a gentle mare, and he gets Devil, a wild-eyed stallion only recently broken sufficiently for rentals. Off they go, and right away he has trouble keeping Devil on the bridle path. Suddenly the horse bucks and only with effort does the rider stay on. "That's one," he says.

A few minutes later, Devil rears up and again the man keeps his saddle only with difficulty. "That's two," the man growls. Finally, as they pass beneath low-lying branches, Devil arches his back and the man's head smacks against a branch.

"That's three!" the man snarls. He dismounts, reaches into his pocket and pulls out a .38 pistol. One shot into Devil's head drops the horse flat on the path.

"What did you do!" his bride screeches. "How could you shoot the poor horse? He was just a bit frisky!"

He turns to her and says, "That's one."

125. Eyes

A man left work on Friday afternoon, but instead of going home, he stayed out the entire weekend hunting with the boys and spending his entire paycheck.

When he finally appeared at home Sunday night, he was confronted by his very angry wife and was barraged for nearly two hours with a tirade. Finally, his wife stopped the yelling and nagging and said to him. "How would you like it if you didn't see me for two or three days?" To which he replied, "That would be fine with me." Monday went by and he didn't see his wife. Tuesday and Wednesday came and went with the same results. Thursday, the swelling went down just enough where he could see her a little out of the corner of his left eye.

MOHEL

(Pronounced MOIL)—a ritual circumcisor. The circumcision is called, in Yiddish, a briss. The thing that is snipped is a penis, a shmeckle, or a putz (depending on one's ethnic background and the situation.)

126. The Circumcision

[Make sure the mohel's name begins with M—that way you won't get confused during the telling. A slight accent is called for, especially the word 'circumcision' should be pronounced 'coicumcision'. This gives the story flavor.]

Jacob and Moishe, young men with an eye to the future, leave Europe and make it to America, to the Lower East Side. Jacob gets a job in a candy store; Moishe becomes a mohel. Jacob marries and in time, his wife presents him with a son. He calls on his old friend to do the honors. Moishe does a fine job and everyone helps himself to a glass of Slivovitz, some herring, a bit of cake. Jacob asks Moishe his fee.

"Ten dollars." Jacob gladly pays.

A few years go by. Jacob has moved up, becoming manager of a small chain of candy stores and now he lives in the Bronx, on the Grand Concourse, in a two bedroom apartment. Again his wife presents him with a son, and again he calls upon Jacob to do the honors. The apartment is filled with friends and neighbors and there's a whole assortment of appetizers, sandwiches from the deli, wines, scotch, soda, cakes....

Moishe does a fine job and when Jacob asks, "How much do I owe you?", says, "Fifty dollars." No problem.

Some years pass. Jacob's chain of stores has been bought out; he's now a vice-president of a large company and living in Larchmont on a two-million dollar estate. Again his wife presents him with a boy and again he calls on his old friend Moishe to be the mohel. To accommodate the large crowd of friends, well-wishers, business acquaintances, etc., a tent has been set up in the back yard. There's a caterer, a sit-down luncheon…the works. At the end, he asks Jacob, "How much do I owe you?"

"Five hundred dollars."

"No problem," but as he's writing out a check, Jacob comments, smiling, "but maybe could you explain your price structure?"

"Of course," Moishe says as he pockets the check. "On the Lower East Side, you had a <u>briss</u>. My fee for a briss is still ten dollars. On the Concourse, you had a <u>coicumcision</u>; my fee for a coicumcision is still fifty dollars. Here, in Larchmont, you had a <u>putzalectamy</u>."

127. Philadelphia

An older man and a man in his late thirties, attending a business convention in New York, are standing beside each other in the Men's Room. The older man, on the left, says to his fellow-pisher,

"You come from Philadelphia, don't you?"

Surprised, the man on the right says,

"Yes. Are you from Phillie?"

"Nope. Haven't been there in twenty years."

"Well, that's amazing. I left Phillie thirty years ago and thought I'd lost whatever accent I had."

"No accent. You lived around Washington Ave?"

"Now I'm astonished!" the man responds. "I was born just two blocks from Washington Ave."

"Your family belonged to Temple Zion."

"What are you, a wizard?"

"No. The Rabbi of Temple Zion was Rabbi Hartz. He was also the mohel. Rabbi Hartz was left-handed and cut on a bias. And you're pissing on my shoes."

128. Clocks

An American traveler is strolling through an old part of Jerusalem, enjoying the charm of the crooked little streets and shops, when he notices that his watch has stopped. Sure enough, there's a store just ahead with a dozen watches and clocks in its window display. He enters the store, removes his watch and hands it over to the proprietor, a small, grey man wearing a yarmulkah.

"My watch stopped," he explains. "Could you take a look at it; maybe it needs a cleaning."

The proprietor shakes his head. "I don't handle from watches," he says in halting English.

"You don't handle watches?" the American repeats. "But your window display...watches and clocks."

"I'm a mohel," the man says. "So what should I put in my window?"

RABBIS

129. Hat

[It is assumed that one knows that a yarmulkah is the skull-cap worn by religious Jews during prayer.]

A rabbi from the old school—black suit; long, black coat; magnificent hat with fur trim is walking along the sidewalk when a gust of wind carries his precious hat into the street...and a bus is bearing down on it! A young man darts into the street and snatches the hat just before the bus crushes it into a ruin. He brushes it off and returns it to its owner, who is so grateful, he asks, "What favor can I do for you?"

"Rabbi," the young man says, "I'm on my way to the track. Bless me, so I'll have a good day."

The rabbi gives him a triple blessing and the young man is off to the racetrack.

First race. There's a horse named <u>Fedora</u>. The rabbi's hat! A Fedora's a hat! He puts ten dollars down on Fedora and Fedora wins easily. Second race...<u>Beret</u>! A beret is also a hat! Forty dollars turns into a hundred fifty. Third race...<u>Topper</u>! Fourth race...<u>Stetson</u>! Every one a winner! <u>Bowler</u>! <u>Tam o'Chanter</u>! <u>Mortarboard</u>! He's got over four thousand of the track's money in his hands but for the eighth race he can't spot the horse! So he puts all four grand on the favorite—My Dream.

My Dream stumbles coming out of the starting gate, throws his jockey and is disqualified. The man sighs and takes the bus home. His wife, preparing supper, asks how it went. He tells her the story.

"And what horse won the eighth race?" she asks.

"Oh, some Japanese nag named...Yarmulkah."

130. Blessing

It's Bernie Schwartz's first visit to the racetrack and he really doesn't know which horse to bet on. He's been warned about the touts and the lineup in the newspaper means nothing to him. He sees a rabbi—short fellow, stout, dressed in a dark suit, black coat, black hat—shuffling over toward the long stable where the horses are kept and decides to follow at a distance. The rabbi walks past horse after horse until he stops, puts both hands on the head of a horse and mutters something. The rabbi then retraces his steps and Bernie follows him to the betting window.

"$10 on the same horse as that guy," Bernie says, pointing to the departing rabbi. The horse wins and again the rabbi is heading toward the stables. Again Bernie follows, sees which horse the rabbi blesses, and Bernie puts his money down. Again the horse wins the race. This happens seven times, and now Bernie has a pocketful of money. Before the eighth race, the rabbi scurries down the row of horses, Bernie following at a distance, until he comes to the last horse, a silver stallion named Competitor. Now the rabbi puts his hands on the horse's head and Bernie can hear him praying...and praying...and praying. What a blessing this one is getting! Bernie doesn't wait; he dashes to the window and puts his entire bundle on Competitor at eight to one odds.

Competitor manages to stagger across the line in a photo-finish for last place. Bernie sees the rabbi leaving the track and catches up to him. "Excuse me," he says, and explains how he'd followed the rabbi and placed his bets.

"So what happened in the eighth race?" he moans. "I mean...after such a blessing!"

"Tell me," the rabbi says. "Are you Jewish?"

"Yeah," Bernie says.

"You go to shul often?"

"Not so much," Bernie admits.

"That's the trouble. You don't know the difference between a <u>Barucha</u> (blessing) and <u>Kaddish</u> (the prayer for the dead.)

131. Pork

A rabbi, wondering why the Christians were so fond of pork, decided to find out for himself what it tasted like. Of course, pork is forbidden to Jews, so he drove two hours, found a restaurant and sitting by himself at a corner table, ordered pork.

Perhaps he was the ten-thousandth customer; perhaps the chef felt chipper that day—in any case, after a considerable wait, the waiter emerged from the kitchen bearing a roast suckling pig with an apple in its mouth.

And just as the waiter approached his table, the door opened and the entire Sisterhood committee from his synagogue, headed by the president's wife, entered. The rabbi jumped to his feet and, waving his hands that they should go back, cried, "You can't eat here! This is a crazy place!" Pointing to the suckling pig, he shouted, "You order a roast apple and look how they serve it!"

132. Poison

An older man enters his rabbi's study early in the morning, closes the door, leans over the rabbi's desk and, sobbing, whispers, "My wife is trying to kill me! By poison yet! It's there on the table, marked Pepper. Rabbi, you've got to do something before I'm a deader!"

The rabbi listens as the man unveils his woe, then asks, "So what do you want me to do? Go to the police?"

"No," he says. "I want you to talk to her. Now, before it's too late. Tell her to stop poisoning me. I'll wait here in your study."

The rabbi agrees to try, and since this takes precedence, immediately goes to the man's house. Time passes. Eleven o'clock. Noon. Three P.M. At five-thirty, the door to the study opens; the rabbi stumbles in, drops into his chair and regards the man tearfully.

"I spoke with her," he says. "She told me her life story. She told me about her mother and father and their life stories. She told me about her alcoholic brother and her rich sister who lives in Scarsdale. She told me of her sacrifices, her sciatica, her menstrual problems, her thinning hair, her lifelong constipation. She talked. And talked."

"But what about the poison?" the man cries.

"My advice to you is, take it," the rabbi says.

133. Not Angry

A congregation in New York honors a Rabbi for 25 years of service by sending him to Hawaii for a week, all-expenses paid. When he walks into his hotel room, there's a beautiful, nude girl lying on the bed.

She says, "Hi, Rabbi, I'm a little something extra that the president of the board paid for!"

The Rabbi is incensed. He picks up the phone, calls the board president and says, "Greenberg, where is your respect? I am the moral leader of our community! As your Rabbi, I am very, very angry with you. You've not heard the end of this!"

The girl gets up and starts to get dressed. The Rabbi turns to her and says, "Where are you going? I'm not angry with you!"

SEX

134. Hammock

At a prestigious golf club, a member gets permission to bring a guest to a tournament. When the guest shows up...not with a bag of clubs but with a baseball bat, a croquet mallet and a pool cue...the Rules Committee meets and only by the most earnest pleading does the member prevent his guest being tossed out. Indeed, they agree to let him make a fool of himself, if he so chooses.

On the first tee, the guest addresses the ball with the croquet mallet and drives it three hundred twenty yards straight down the fairway. It's a dogleg, with a screen of birch trees hiding the green. Using the baseball bat, he whacks the ball over the trees and onto the green. One shot with the pool cue and the ball travels a tortuous path directly into the cup. In the end, he wins the tournament easily and gets a hole-in-one, to boot.

When you get a hole-in-one, you buy drinks for the house. He asks the bartender to set out glasses in a row and to give him a pitcher of martini and a shot glass. Standing with his back to the bar, he repeatedly fills the shot glass, tosses the drink over his shoulder and fills each glass in turn without spilling a drop.

By this time, there's a reporter present. The reporter takes him aside and asks him what's going on here. Is it a trick?

"No," the fellow replies. "I just happen to have unusual dexterity; what for most folks is a challenge, to me is simple. So I always give away odds. I play ping-pong with a tennis racquet, tennis with a ping-pong paddle, etc."

"Wow!" exclaims the reporter, making notes. "Tell me…how do you…how do you…?"

"Don't be embarrassed; everyone asks the same question. Standing up in a hammock."

135. Great Neck

At the water cooler in a Manhattan office, Joe complains to his co-worker Dave about his lack of love life. Dave smiles knowingly and says in a low voice, "Listen up, buddy. After work, go to Penn Station and take a train that goes to Great Neck. Get off at Great Neck. You'll see a bunch of women who've driven down to pick up their husbands. Some of the men won't show and the wives have to drive home alone. Likely they have dinner on the table and they're feeling sorry for themselves. Take your pick, talk to her a little; odds are she'll invite you back for dinner and who knows what else! Eh?" With a wink.

Joe finds the Great Neck train, but falls asleep and doesn't wake until the train pulls in at Port Washington, the end of the line. He gets off, and finds that it's exactly as Dave said. Soon most of the cars leave, but one remains, with an attractive brunette behind the wheel. He walks over, starts a conversation and sure enough, is invited back for dinner. Afterwards, they decide to skip dessert and head upstairs. They are entertaining each other mightily when suddenly the door bursts open and there's the husband, in a rage.

"What the hell!" is for openers, and for five minutes he curses his wife. Then he looks at Joe and roars, "And as for you, shmuck, I told you to get off at Great Neck!"

136. Minsk

A young Jewish man from Minsk goes to his rabbi with the following problem. "For six weeks I'm married to a wonderful woman. She's beautiful, a wonderful cook, handles the money fine, keeps the house clean...but every time we go to bed together, it's inside, outside, upside downside, forward and backward! I don't understand this."

The rabbi pulls out three volumes of the Talmud and studies them for a half-hour. Then, replacing them, he turns to the man and pronounces, "This is a violation of Torah! Immediate divorce!"

<u>Like a stab in the heart!</u> But to divorce such a wonderful wife...the man decides to travel to Pinsk, to see the rabbi there. After half a day on the train, and waiting for an appointment, he is ushered into the rabbi's study. "Rabbi," he says, "I'm from Minsk. For six weeks I'm married to a wonderful woman. She's beautiful, a wonderful cook, handles the money fine, keeps the house clean...but every time we go to bed together, it's inside, outside, upside downside, forward and backward! I don't understand this."

The rabbi lays out six volumes of the Talmud, studies them for two hours, then looks up and says, "This is an abomination! A sacrilege! Immediate divorce!"

<u>A stab in the heart and a kick in the stomach!</u> The poor wretch stumbles out of the study and walks the streets of Pinsk for hours. What to do? He prays and the answer comes to him...he will journey to Warsaw and get an appointment with the Chief Rabbi.

After two days on the train and two more waiting for a few minutes with the sage, he is admitted to the rabbi's booklined study. This is an old man, with a long, white beard and eyes rheumy from a lifetime of study. Seated in an armchair, surrounded by books, he motions the visitor to a chair. "Rabbi," the young man whispers, "I'm from Minsk. For six weeks I'm married to a wonderful woman. She's beautiful, a wonderful cook, handles the money fine, keeps the house clean...but every time we go to bed together, it's inside, outside, upside downside, forward and backward! I don't understand. Now I'll tell you...I already went to the rabbis of Minsk and Pinsk and they both said, Immediate Divorce! What you declare is what I'll do."

The rabbi leans back in his chair, grabs his beard with both hands and roars with laughter. "The rabbis of Minsk and Pinsk! These are young <u>pishers</u> right from the seminary! What do they know from fancy fucking?"

137. Paint

It's late Friday afternoon. A young man is in a bar, having a drink after a hard day's work. He's not looking forward to the weekend. A woman comes up to him and takes the initiative. "Come on up to my place and I'll show you a great time. I'll do anything you want for a hundred dollars."

"Not interested, ma'am," he says.

"Anything!" she insists. "Only a hundred dollars! Anything... you...want!"

"Really?" he asks. "Anything?"

"Anything!"

Off they go and soon they're in her apartment and she's removing her clothes. After applying some dabs of perfume, she stands in front of him and, wearing only a hard smile, says, "Anything!"

He reaches into his wallet, removes five twenty-dollar bills, hands them over. "Anything, you said. Right?"

"Anything, dearie."

"Good. Get dressed and come with me. You're going to paint my apartment."

138. Porch

A blonde decides to earn some money doing handy work, so she goes to an affluent part of town and knocks on the first door. A man answers. "Is there any work you need done?" she asks.

"Yep," says the man. "My porch needs a painting. How much will you charge?"

She thinks, then says, "Fifty dollars."

"Okay. The paint and brushes are in the garage. Let me know when you're finished."

As he closes the door behind him, his wife says, "I heard what that girl is charging. Does she realize the porch goes all around the house?"

Smugly, her husband says, "Well, she's a professional; she should know what she's bidding on."

An hour later the doorbell rings and the blonde announces that the job is finished. "And I had enough paint for two coats. And it's not a porch; it's a Lexus."

139. Stronger

A white-haired gentleman enters a doctor's office, strips and seats himself on the examination table. Twenty minutes later, having passed all the tests, he is pronounced healthy. "Is there anything you'd like to ask?" the doctor says.

"Yes. When I was twenty and had an erection, it was so stiff I couldn't bend it even a little. When I was fifty, I could bend it maybe half an inch. Now that I'm seventy, I can bend it all the way back.

"Doctor," he whispers with a smile, "am I getting stronger?"

140. Schmaltz

Three men were discussing their sex lives.

The Italian said, "Last week my wife and I had great sex. I rubbed her body all over with olive oil, we made passionate love and she screamed for five minutes!"

The Frenchman boasted, "Last week my wife and I had sex, also. I rubbed her body all over with tub butter fresh from the creamery and laced with cognac; then we made love and she screamed for fifteen minutes!"

The Jewish man said, "Well, last week my wife and I had sex, too. I rubbed her body all over with chicken shmaltz (kosher chicken fat), we made love and she screamed for six hours!"

The Italian and Frenchman were stunned. "What could you have possibly done to make your wife scream for six hours?"

"I wiped my hands on her new drapes."

141. The Eye

A man is dining in a fancy restaurant and can hardly keep his eyes off a gorgeous redhead sitting at the next table. Suddenly she sneezes and her glass eye comes flying out towards the man. He reflexively reaches out, grabs it out of the air and hands it back.

"Oh, my, I am sooo sorry," the woman says as she discretely turns away to pop the eye back into place. "Let me buy your dinner to make it up to you." They enjoy a wonderful dinner together and afterwards they take in a movie followed by drinks. They laugh, talk, share dreams and after paying for everything, she invites him back to her place for a nightcap, and to stay for breakfast.

The next morning, she prepares a delicious omelet, with juice, toast and fresh coffee. "You know," says the man, "you are the perfect woman. Are you this nice to every guy you meet?"

"No," she replies…"you happened to catch my eye."

142. The Stutterer

[Don't overdo the stuttering...just enough to get the idea across. Get the punch line out quickly.]

A strapping young man in his doctor's office complains:

"Doc, Y...y...you've got to d...do something ab...about my st...stutt...stuttering! It's driv...driving my wi...wife crazy!"

The doctor gives him a thorough physical and then explains, "The reason for your stuttering is that your penis is unusually large and heavy and it's pulling down on your central nervous system, which affects your vocal apparatus at the other end. Let me cut out a three-inch section and I guarantee your stuttering will stop.

"Gr...great! Go ah...ahead, doc!"

The operation is performed and the man recovers nicely at home. Two weeks later, he returns to the doctor's office for a follow-up and says, "Doc, you're the best diagnostician I've ever met. I went to three other doctors, and none of them could figure out what was causing my stuttering. I have more confidence; my job performance has improved a hundred percent...but I have a problem. My wife isn't happy. She wants those three inches back and she'll live with the stuttering."

The doctor says, "W...well, it's a b...bit la...late for th...that!"

[If this goes over well, you may segue into the following, which should be tossed out quickly:]

Two guys who haven't seen each other for years meet on the street. "How you doing, Joe?"

"Just fine. I'm a s...sales manager now."

"Hey, your stuttering's a lot better than it used to be. How about your sister? She had a worse problem than you."

"Oh, it's as b...bad as ever. Last month she went out with a f...fellow and by the time she could s...say she wasn't th...that kind of...girl.... <u>she was</u>."

143. Deaf Wife

[This is a quickie. As a raconteur, use this only to gain entree for longer, more elaborate stories.]

"Did you hear about the woman who had ten children because she was mostly deaf?"

"No."

"Every night her husband asked, 'Do you want to go to sleep, or what?' And she replied, 'What?'"

144. Password

A woman was helping her computer-illiterate husband set up his computer and as the final step, told him that he would now have to select a password.

The husband, in an amorous mood, typed in P-E-N-I-S.

His wife fell off her chair laughing when the computer replied: "PASSWORD REJECTED—NOT LONG ENOUGH".

145. The Magic Towel

[Great story. Tell this with enthusiasm.]

An old Jewish man married a young woman but found that she was never able to achieve orgasm when they made love. This is contrary to the Jewish ideal, so they went to a rabbi. After listening to their plight, the rabbi said:

"Hire a young man to stand over you when you're making love and wave a towel. Your wife will fantasize and achieve pleasure."

They did as he'd said, hiring a handsome bodybuilder, who dutifully waved a towel over them as they lay in bed, flipping it this way and that way. But in the end, still the wife was left out! They went back to the rabbi, who thought a while, then said:

"This time, you stand over the bed and let the young man be your surrogate; as he makes love to your wife, you wave the towel!"

They did as the rabbi ordered. The husband swept the air back and forth and snapped the towel, <u>crack!</u> <u>crack!</u> while the young stud went to work with passion and vigor and lifted the wife to screaming heights of sexual glory. When the act was over, the old man tapped the surrogate on the shoulder and said, smiling, "You see, <u>that's</u> how one waves a towel properly!"

146. Brand New

A young fellow standing in the fairway is hit by a golf ball right in the cojones and goes down in agony. Later, after he's recovered, he goes to the doctor.

"Well, you sure took a shot, son," the doctor says. "I'm going to put it in a splint."

"But I'm getting married next week!" the fellow cries. "My fiancee hasn't...won't...never...."

"Don't worry, son," the doctor reassures him. "By next week, you can take the splint off and it should be just as good as new." And with that, he takes four tongue depressors and gently wraps and tapes the fellow's penis on all four sides.

After the wedding, the couple go off to the bridal suite of the local hotel. She removes her clothing and, facing him, displays her rather magnificent breasts proudly, saying, "You see these? No man has ever touched them!"

Smiling, he removes his undershorts and says, "You see this? It's still in the crate!"

147. Hello

Sonia, a widow, is sitting by the telephone when it rings. "Hello," she says.

A deep male voice replies, "How would you like it if I came over, ripped off your blouse and bra, stripped away your skirt and panties and made violent love to you for an hour?"

She says, "From just 'hello' you can tell all this?"

148. Party

A couple was invited to a swanky masked Halloween party. She got a terrible headache and told her husband to go to the party alone. He, being a devoted husband, protested, but she argued and said she was going to take some aspirin and go to bed, and there was no need for his good time to be spoiled by not going. So he took his costume and away he went. The wife, after sleeping soundly for about an hour, awakened without pain, and, as it was still early, decided to go to the party. Inasmuch as her husband did not know what her costume was, she thought she would have some fun by watching her husband to see how he acted when she was not with him. She joined the party and soon spotted her husband cavorting around on the dance floor, dancing with every nice chick he could and copping a little feel here and a little kiss there. His wife went up to him and being a rather seductive babe herself, he left his partner high and dry and devoted his time to the new stuff that had just arrived. She let him go as far as he wished, naturally, since he was her husband. Finally he whispered a little proposition in her ear and she agreed, so off they went to one of the cars and had a good time. Just before unmasking at midnight, she slipped away and went home and put the costume away and got into bed, wondering what kind of explanation he would make for his behavior. She was sitting up reading when he came in and asked what kind of a time he had. He said, "Oh, the same old thing. You know I never have a good time when you're not there." Then she asked, "Did you dance much?" He replied, "I'll tell you, I never even danced one dance. When I got there, I met Pete, Bill Brown and some other guys, so we went into the den and played poker all evening. But you're not going to believe what happened to the guy I loaned my costume to!"

149. On The Road to Inverness

One misty Scottish morning a man is driving through the hills to Inverness. Suddenly out of the mist, a massive red-haired highlander steps into the middle of the road. The man is at least six feet four and has a huge red beard and, despite the wind, mist and near freezing temperatures, is wearing only his kilt, a tweed shirt and a tam-o'-shanter at a rakish angle. At the roadside there also stands a young woman. She is absolutely beautiful—slim, shapely, fair complexion, golden hair…heart stopping. The driver stops and stares, and his attention is only distracted from the lovely girl when the red thing opens the car door and drags him from his seat onto the road with a fist resembling a whole raw ham.

"Right, you Jimmy," shouts the highlander, "Ah want you to masturbate!"

"But…" stammers the driver.

"Du it now—or I'll bluddy kill yu!" So the driver turns his back on the girl, drops his trousers and starts to masturbate. Thinking of the girl on the roadside this doesn't take him long.

"Right!" snarls the Highlander "Du it agin!"

"But….." says the driver.

"Now!" So the driver does it again.

"Right laddie, du it agin!" demands the Highlander. The hapless driver gets cramps in both arms, he has rubbed himself raw, has violent knob-ache, his sight is failing (as promised for years by his priest) and despite the cold wind has collapsed in a sweating, gibbering heap on the ground, unable to stand.

"Du it again!" says the Highlander.

"I can't do it any more! You'll just have to kill me!" whimpers the man.

The Highlander looks down at the pathetic soul slumped on the roadside. "All right laddie." he says, "NOW, can you give ma daughter a lift to Inverness?"

150. Brothel

Two Irishmen were sitting in a pub with their beers and a clear view of the brothel across the street. As they observed a baptist minister enter the house one of them said, "Aye, 'tis a shame to see a man of the cloth goin' bad."

Shortly after, a rabbi went into the brothel. The other Irishman said, "Aye, 'tis a shame to see that the Jews are fallin' victim to temptation."

Then a Catholic priest came along and entered the brothel. One of the Irishmen said, "What a terrible pity…one of the girls must be quite ill."

SOPHISTICATED STORIES

[These require the right audience, one prepared to hang on every word; not suitable for noisy parties, etc.]

151. Bohr

A reporter, interviewing the famed physicist Niels Bohr, noticed a horseshoe over the door of his study. "How can a man of science believe in the magic good luck powers of a horseshoe?" he asked.

"I don't," Bohr replied.

"Then why do you have it?"

"I understand that it brings good luck even if you don't believe in it."

152. Anthology

Three dons from Cambridge University, dining out, were discussing the names of categories of things, such as a <u>pod</u> of whales, an <u>exaltation</u> of larks and the like. Upon emerging into the street, they spy a group of ladies of the night strolling around a lamppost.

"What name would you give to that collection?" asks the senior don?

"A jam of tarts," ventures the most junior don.

"A flurry of strumpets," suggests the other don.

"Hm. No...I think...an anthology of pros," the senior don decides.

153. Big John

[This story illustrates the fact that everything is relative. In fact, it is a good preface to a study of Einstein's theory. Even if it won't help one understand the complexities...it can't hurt.]

A New Yorker is driving out west on vacation and comes to a small, quiet town in the hills of Colorado. Stepping into a bar, he engages the bartender in conversation. "Is this town always so quiet?"

"Well, sure," the bartender says, wiping a glass. "The big event here is the annual Rotary Club picnic. That's about it...'cept when Big John hits town. Then everyone clears out."

"Big John?" says the New Yorker.

"Yup. You don't wanna be caught here when Big John comes into town."

Just then the door bursts open and a man yells in, "Big John's comin'! Big John's comin'!"

He vanishes and the New Yorker finds himself alone in the bar; the bartender having taken a dive. Well, this sounds interesting; the New Yorker waits to see what'll happen next.

A few minutes later there's a snorting and grunting outside and the New Yorker sees a large, barrel-chested man ride up to the bar on a bull, bareback. Sliding off the animal, the man roars, "Stay!" and the bull paws the ground, but nods. The man strides into the bar, slams his fist down and roars, "Whiskey!"

The bartender emerges from his hiding place, hands over a pint of whiskey and vanishes.

The man opens the bottle by smashing its neck against the bar, tilts his head back and gurgles down the entire pint. The New Yorker, wide-eyed, asks, "Do you always drink so...fast?"

"No," the man says with a glance at the door. "But I gotta hurry; Big John's coming!"

154. Beethoven's Ninth

[This one requires practice!]

It is reported that in performances of Beethoven's ninth symphony, the base viols don't play a note until the fourth movement. Prior to a performance, the senior bassist suggests to the other four that they repair to the bar across the street for a couple of beers, which they do.

After three beers, the most junior bassist suggests they get back. "Oh, they can't start the fourth movement without us," the senior player says. "I took strong music wire and tied down the fourth movement on the podium with a tricky knot; I'll have plenty of time to untie it while the chorus moves into position." With that, he orders another round of beer, and then another. When that is finished, the five of them weave their way across the street, into the music hall and, with some wobbling, into their seats, where two of them immediately nod off.

The conductor regards their entrance with a cold eye and at the end of the third movement looks at the knotted score, puts down his baton, turns to the audience and announces,

"It's the bottom of the ninth, the score is tied, the bases are loaded and there are two out."

155. Lord & Taylor

The sign outside his little shop in Minsk read:<u>Rabinowitz, Tailor</u>.
[Move your hand through the air, <u>showing</u> your listeners that sign.]
Young Rabinowitz, anxious to build up a trade, worked very hard, yet was generous to the poor, found time to study Torah and Talmud and, in short was a credit to the Jewish community. One evening, working late, he heard a voice. A commanding voice.
"Rabinowitz...it's time to move. Go to Warsaw."

There was no prankster in the shop; the door was locked. Could it be....? Rabinowitz looked up and saw an ethereal glow. It <u>had</u> to be a direct order from the Lord!

It took him two weeks to close up his shop, into which he'd poured sweat and tears, but he had to obey. He moved to Warsaw, opened a larger shop, worked even longer hours, yet found time for the good deeds that were an integral part of his character. His shop prospered and again the sign outside read:

Rabinowitz, Tailor.

He married and in time became a father. And then, one night as he worked, he again heard a voice. "Rabinowitz…it's time to move. Go to America."

After all the effort of building up his clientele all over…but when the Lord God says go, one obeys! Rabinowitz sold out and, with his wife and child, took a boat to America, settling on the Lower East Side of Manhattan. He opened a tailor shop, larger than the one in Warsaw, took English lessons at night, continued his contributions to the community and prospered. And again the sign outside his shop read:

Rabinowitz, Tailor.

Rabinowitz began selling clothing, expanded his store, hired personnel, expanded again and became prosperous, yet never forgot to provide for the poor or to skip his study of the Torah and Talmud. And then one night, as in a dream, came the command: "Rabinowitz…move to Fifth Avenue. I will lead you."

One obeys, and over the next year, Rabinowitz, with an architectural firm, took over a building, created and built a store larger than any for a mile around. On the day before the store was to open, he went to his synagogue and prayed fervently:

"Lord, as Thou has said, so have I done, and I have become wealthy beyond my dreams. You are my partner in all that I have accomplished. Let me honor Thee by naming the store: God and Rabinowitz."

"Nay," came the reply, gentle as a dove's flight. "Name it...<u>Lord and Taylor</u>."

156. Encore

The operagoers at La Scala, in Milan, Italy, are demanding. When a young tenor made his debut as Rhadames in Aida, he struggled from the first note and as the opera progressed, his voice wavered and shrank. But at the completion of a major aria, the house rose and cheered.

"Encore!" they shouted.

He croaked his way through a second rendition of the aria but could go no further when the operagoers again rose and shouted, "Encore! Encore!"

The manager came out onto the stage and, smiling nervously, said, "Thank you, but we must proceed with the opera!"

An old man in the balcony rose and shouted, "<u>He'll sing it until he sings it right</u>!"

157. Shakespeare

[This one requires pencil and paper.]

A troupe of actors was touring England doing Shakespeare in repertory. The advance man went ahead to the next town to arrange for publicity, and told the sign-maker that he needed to advertise six plays on one placard, but it shouldn't look messy or cluttered. When he came back the next day, the sign-maker showed him his sign:
[Write this out just as shown:]

Miscarriage

Wet   Dry

3"   6"   9"

"And what's that supposed to mean?" demanded the advance man.
[Point to each item, starting from the top.]
"Love's Labor Lost", the sign-maker explained.
"Midsummer Night's Dream" "Twelfth Night"
"Much Ado about Nothing"
      "As You Like It"
           "The Taming of the Shrew"

WOMEN

158. The Tenth Bird

At the bar of a transoceanic liner are three women from New York City. The first, a frosted blonde, drapes her hand on the bar, revealing a ring with a huge stone. "This is my travelling diamond," she says. "My jeweler tells me that salt air damages the settings so I keep my better jewelry in the vault."

"Salt air!" sniffs the second lady, pulling a fur jacket around her shoulders. "I wouldn't think of taking my ermine dinner-wrap to sea; I make do with my mink."

The third woman sighs and admits, "I haven't got such jewelry or furs, but my husband has a <u>shmeckle</u> so long and hard that ten birds can stand on it at the same time."

That ends the conversation. Five minutes later, the vessel hits an iceberg and after a lot of screaming and rushing, the same three women find themselves alone in a lifeboat.

"It's my fault!" wails the blonde. "It's God's punishment for lying! This isn't a diamond; it's a rhinestone I bought for less than forty dollars!"

The second lady, bawling and tearing at her hair, screeches, "What have I done? What have I done? That's not a mink...it's dyed squirrel I bought from a second-hand store on Pitkin Avenue!"

The third woman is bent over, racked with sobs. "No, no. It's me, it's all me. The truth is...the tenth bird has to stand on one leg."

159. Confessions

Four ladies finish their game of canasta and as they enjoy coffee and cake, one of them says, "You know, ladies, we've been playing canasta for ten years and...I have a confession to make. I think you should know...I'm a kleptomaniac. But I'd never take anything from you!"

A second woman, smiling, puts down her coffeecup and slyly says, "Well, as long as we're confessing, maybe I should tell you...I'm a nymphomaniac. But I've never made a move on your husbands. Never!"

The third woman hesitates, then says slowly, "Well...even my husband doesn't know this...but I'm a closet lesbian. But I've never approached any of you, nor would I."

The fourth woman, rising, says, "As long as we're sharing...I'm a gossip...and I've got to get to a phone!"

160. Vase

Two women have driven to the suburban train station and are awaiting the arrival of their husbands. The train pulls in and two men get off together. One of them is carrying a bouquet of flowers.

"Oh, no!" cries one of the women. "Now I'm going to have to spend the whole weekend with my legs in the air!"

"How uncomfortable!" asks the other. "Don't you have a vase?"

161. My God

Four Catholic women who have just become acquainted are having coffee and chatting. One of them announces, with unconcealed pride, "You'll want to know that my son just became a priest! Now, when people talk to him, it's <u>Father</u> Molloy!"

Mrs. Flaherty smiles and says, "Well, my son is a Bishop and when people talk to him, it's <u>Your Grace</u>!"

Mrs. Ryan glances at the others and says, with justifiable pride, "My son is Cardinal Ryan, of Boston. When people speak to him, it's <u>Your Eminence</u>!"

The fourth woman nods and says, "Well, my son is a six-foot two bodybuilder who does modelling. When the girls look at him, all they can say is, <u>My God</u>!"

162. Ladies' Night Out

Two women are jealous of their husbands' 'night out with the boys'. They don't know how to play poker so they do the next best thing, go out one evening to a bar and get themselves rather plastered on beer. By the time the bar closes, the busses have stopped running and they have to walk home. As they pass a cemetery, they become aware of a need to pee. They have no choice; they slip behind some tombstones and relieve themselves.

The first woman, finding herself without anything to clean herself with, removes her panties, uses and discards them. The second woman, unwilling to do that, uses the ribbon of a flower wreath.

The morning after, one husband phones the other. "We'd better stop this," he says. "My wife came home without her panties."

The other husband responded, "You're lucky. Mine came home with a card stuck to her ass that read, 'We will never forget you.'"

163. In the Pond

[To be told with a gleam in the eye.]

An old farmer had owned a large farm for several years. He had a large pond in the back, fixed up nice; picnic tables, horseshoe courts, basketball court, etc. The pond was properly shaped and fixed up for swimming when it was built.

One evening the old farmer decided to go down to the pond, as he hadn't been there for a while, and look it over. As he neared the pond, he heard voices shouting and laughing with glee. As he came closer he saw it was a bunch of young women skinny dipping in his pond.

He made the women aware of his presence and they all went to the deep end of the pond. One of the women shouted to him,

"We're not coming out until you leave!"

The old man replied, "I didn't come down here to watch you ladies swim or make you get out of the pond naked.

"I only came to feed the alligator."

Moral: Old age and treachery will triumph over youth and skill.

164. Brains

In the hospital the relatives gathered in the waiting room, where their family member lay gravely ill. Finally, the doctor came in looking tired and somber.

"I'm afraid I'm the bearer of bad news," he said as he surveyed the worried faces. "The only hope left for your loved one at this time is a brain transplant. It's an experimental procedure, very risky and you will have to pay for the brain yourselves."

The family members sat silent as they absorbed the news. After a length of time, someone asked,

"Well, how much does a brain cost?"

The doctor quickly responded, "$5,000 for a male brain, and "$200 for a female brain."

The moment turned awkward. Men in the room tried not to smile, avoiding eye contact with the women, but some actually smirked. A man, unable to control his curiosity, blurted out the question everyone wanted to ask,

"Why is the male brain so much more?"

The doctor smiled at the childish innocence and so to the entire group hesaid, "It's just standard pricing procedure. We have to mark down the price of the female brains, because they've been used."

165. Navajo Woman

A saleswoman is driving home in Northern Arizona when she sees a Navajo woman hitchhiking. Because the trip has been long and boring, she stops the car and the Navajo woman climbs in.

During their small talk, the Navajo woman glances surreptitiously at a brown bag on the front seat between them. If you're wondering what's in the bag," offers the saleswoman, "it's a bottle of wine. I got it for my husband."

The Navajo woman is silent for a while, nods several times and says, "Good trade."

166. A Perfect Tan

A well-proportioned secretary, Yolanda, spent the day sunbathing on the roof of her hotel, wearing a bikini. The next day, realizing that she was alone on the roof and no one could see her, she decided to sunbathe au natural, for a more even tan. She'd hardly begun when she heard someone running up the stairway; as she was lying on her stomach, she just pulled a towel over her rear.

"Excuse me, miss," said the flustered little assistant manager, out of breath. "We don't mind you sunbathing on the roof, but I must insist that you wear your bathing suit as you did yesterday.

"Who cares?" Yolanda asked. "No one can see me up here and besides, I'm covered with a towel."

"Not exactly," the manager replied. "You're lying on the dining room skylight."

167. Devotion

Three women are bragging about their devoted sons.

Mrs. Cohen says, "My son is so devoted, he bought me a trip around the world, first class!"

Mrs. Lapidus counters, "Mine is more devoted! For my birthday, he rented a banquet hall, hired a nine-piece band and catered a party for all my old friends from Brooklyn!"

Mrs. Fine laughed. "You want to hear devoted? Three times a week my son goes to a psychiatrist. A hundred twenty dollars an hour he pays! And who does he talk about the whole time? ME!"

EPILOGUE

So here you are. Some of these stories may appeal to you more than others. Take those that you like and practice telling them until you have them down cold. The next time you're standing around with a group, perhaps with a cold gin-and-tonic in your hand, wait for a natural break in the conversation, then slip in a short one. Don't follow immediately with another; be polite. Perhaps someone has a natural follow-up to yours. Remember it; add it to your repertoire, which will grow.

Oh…the mouse and the elephant. I almost forgot. The elephant had just emitted a loud grunt as the coconut fell on her head. The mouse disengaged himself, ran along her back and spoke into her ear: "Did I hurt you, bubbie?"

*   *   *

Some of you with a taste for modern fantasy might enjoy one of my novels—The Inn at the End of the World, or its sequel, The Devil's Grandmother. Descriptive blurbs are provided on the next two pages, and are available at the publishers' websites (Xlibris and iUniverse, respectively), or at the websites of Amazon, Borders or Barnes & Noble.

The Inn at the End of the World
by Gene Levin
pub: XLibris

It all starts with God's aunt.

You didn't know the Lord God had an aunt?

She wanders the Earth, carrying a sack into which she pops the curses and maledictions that spout from the mouths of humankind like the vile emanations of a volcano. This, lest the flood of abominations reach her Nephew's ears and rouse sorrow and anger in Him.

Overhearing a morsel of wisdom from Myron Blunger, she attempts to relay it Upstairs, but her aim is bad and the keeper of the Inn at the End of the World learns the whereabouts of Blunger....

Yes, the Inn at the End of the World. That's the final abode of fictional characters who have maintained a readership. Holmes and Watson reside there, as do Long John Silver, Cinderella, Don Quixote and many, many others, including Joey Willem, a ten-year-old boy created by this same Blunger.

Joey has stolen the Innkeeper's seven-league boots! Now the Innkeeper has Blunger, an overweight, retired librarian, kidnapped from his two bedroom apartment in the Bronx and brought to the Inn so he can write Joey back...with the boots!

That he put forth a sincere effort, he is to put himself into the storyline.

The sequence of adventures Blunger finds himself enmeshed in would freeze the heart and kishkes of the bulliest, most strapping, red-headed adventurer ever to buckle a swash.

In the Grand Finale, he finds himself belly-down on a rocky plateau between the Dromedary Mountains, facing the invasion of Earth by Wotan, Loki, Frost giants, goblins and the like, with a flesh-eating leech eating at his rump. He cries for aid, which arrives from a most unexpected source.

Copies can be ordered from the XLibris website, or by calling 1-888-795-4274 or through any bookstore.

The Devil's Grandmother
by Gene Levin
pub: iUniverse

Does romance stand a chance between the Devil's Grandmother and Vlad the Impaler, given her age (4000 years) and his tendency to skewer those who disagree with him? But first Vlad must be expelled from hell, which is fine with Satan; Vlad refuses to accept his ordained purge until he has revenged himself on the Blungers and this is unhinging the smooth running of the underworld. But his expulsion requires the Lord God's okay.

Satan devises a beautiful scheme. His beloved grandmother will find happiness. Vlad will leave hell and become dean of students at Fairweather College. Vlad is to preach to the sinful students and administrators of that place. Should the students continue in their lustful and slothful ways, they will be brought down to hell en masse. If Vlad succeeds in reforming them, he will remain as Dean. Either way, Satan wins.

And, to make it even more interesting, a Blunger is teaching at that very college. A Blunger of the family against whom Vlad harbors a five-hundred year old grudge! The son of the Blunger whom the Lord God ordered to lost twenty pounds, and who has instead gained eleven!

What a coup for Satan to bring a Blunger down! A Blunger? Why not all of them!

Copies can be ordered from the iUniverse website, or by calling 1-877-823-9235 or through any bookstore.

Made in the USA
Lexington, KY
15 April 2014